UNDERSTANDING SHINTO

Origins • Beliefs • Practices
Festivals • Spirits • Sacred Places

UNDERSTANDING SHINTO

Origins • Beliefs • Practices
Festivals • Spirits • Sacred Places

C. Scott Littleton

DUNCAN BAIRD PUBLISHERS
LONDON

Understanding Shinto
C. Scott Littleton

First published in the United Kingdom and Ireland in 2002 by
Duncan Baird Publishers Ltd
Sixth Floor
Castle House
75–76 Wells Street
London W1T 3QH

Conceived, created and designed by Duncan Baird Publishers

Project Editor: Christopher Westhorp
Senior Editor: Diana Loxley
Design: Cobalt id
Picture Researcher: Julia Ruxton

British Library Cataloguing-in-Publication Data:
A CIP record for this book is available from the British Library

ISBN-10: 1-84483-199-X ISBN-13: 9-781844-831999

10 9 8 7 6 5 4 3 2 1

Typeset in Garamond Three
Colour reproduction by Scanhouse, Malaysia
Printed and bound in Singapore by Imago

NOTES
The abbreviations BCE and CE are used throughout this book:
BCE Before the Common Era (the equivalent of BC)
CE Common Era (the equivalent of AD)

Page 2: The Akino Miyajima Great *Torii* rises out of the sea near the Itsukushima shrine, which is dedicated to the daughters of the storm god Susano.

CONTENTS

INTRODUCTION

The inhabitants of Japan simultaneously espouse two major faiths, Shinto and Buddhism, which have coexisted and influenced one another for the past fifteen hundred years. Shinto is indigenous to Japan and, although stripped of the privileged status it enjoyed from 1868 until the end of the Second World War in 1945, the religion still permeates almost every aspect of Japanese life.

The reverence shown by the Japanese toward nature stems from Shinto's most ancient and fundamental belief that spirit-beings govern the natural world. These spirits, or deities, are known as *kami* (see pp.24–5)—the religion itself is called the "Way of the Gods (or Spirits)," which is expressed both by the native phrase *Kami no Michi* and the synonymous term Shinto, a Japanese articulation of the Chinese *shen* ("spirit") and *dao* ("way"). Both phrases are written with the Chinese characters for *shen* and *dao*. Shinto has been the more usual expression since the resurgence of the religion in the eighteenth and nineteenth centuries—an irony, since the promoters of the revival tended to be anti-Chinese.

Shinto, unlike Buddhism or Christianity, has no known founder. It was not until the late prehistoric Yayoi culture (ca. 300BCE–300CE) that features emerged that are reminiscent of some of the religion's central aspects (for example, the *kami*). Archaic Shinto seems to have evolved by the beginning of the final phase of Japanese prehistory, the Kofun, or "Tumulus," era (ca. 300–550CE). This belief system was intensely local, focusing on the spiritual power inherent in nearby topographical features and on the divine ancestors of clans and lineages. As the Yamato ("Sun") clan gained influence over the others, its divine ancestor, the sun goddess Amaterasu (see pp.28–30), rose to prominence. This laid the foundations for the emperor cult, which was relegated to a symbolic role during the reign of the shoguns (in the twelfth to nineteenth centuries), but returned to dominate Shinto in modern times.

In the mid-sixth century CE, Buddhism was brought to Japan from China via Korea. Confucianism and Daoism also made their appearance in Japan in this period. All three religions, but particularly Buddhism, had a distinct influence on Shinto—the line between Buddhism and Shintoism can sometimes be hazy: for example, many Buddhist deities came to be worshiped as Shinto *kami*. But despite the impact of Chinese belief and philosophy, Japan always remained distinct from its neighbor across the sea. The nation's deep-rooted tendency to adapt and transform what it borrows from other cultures manifested itself, and many Buddhist sects that took root or emerged in Japan soon became, and have remained, uniquely Japanese.

In 1868, after more than 250 years of rule by the Tokugawa shogunate, the Meiji restoration returned power to the emperor (enthroned in 1867), and in 1871

Worshipers bow before a Shinto shrine at Karatsu on Kyushu island during the annual Kunchi festival, held in November.

Shinto was established as the state religion. Along with the newly instituted imperial army and navy, "State Shinto" became a principal mechanism for fostering Japanese nationalism and loyalty to the emperor. The word "Shinto" dates from this period—before this time, the religion was simply the worship of the *kami*.

"State Shinto" came to an abrupt end with the conclusion of the Second World War in 1945. The emperor renounced all claims to divinity, and Japan's post-war constitution of 1947 specifically prohibited the state from having any involvement in religious affairs. As a result of these changes, Shinto reverted to what it had been for most of its long history: a loosely organized collection of local *jinja* ("shrines") dedicated to an almost infinite number of *kami* who, for the most part, were unique to their local communities.

In more recent years, Japan has witnessed the establishment of the so-called "New Religions" (see pp.100–103), and the reemergence of Christianity, which reached Japan in the sixteenth century but was subsequently suppressed. The growth of these faiths was stimulated respectively by the social chaos of the last three decades (1838–67) of the Tokugawa shogunate and by the rapid economic development that followed the Second World War. But in each case, the end result has been quintessentially Japanese, a relatively seamless blend of foreign and indigenous ideas, customs, rites, and beliefs.

Syncretism (the fusion of disparate beliefs and practices into a single system) has long been a feature of religious life in Japan, together with what in the West might be considered a high degree of "ambiguity tolerance." With some important exceptions, most Japanese people would probably consider themselves to be both Shintoists and Buddhists and would perceive no contradiction in practicing two faiths with such radically different roots. Broadly speaking, Shinto focuses on matters relating to this world, on procreation, the promotion of fertility, on spiritual purity, and physical well-being. Buddhism, on the other hand, although it does not reject the real world, has always placed greater emphasis on salvation and the possibility of an afterlife—hence it is often associated with human concerns over mortality and most Japanese prefer its funeral practices.

Any assessment of the role played by religion in ancient or modern Japan must take into account certain fundamental aspects of Japanese culture. Most important is the subordination of the individual to the group, epitomized in the Japanese expression, "the nail that sticks up will be hammered down." Many scholars believe that this ethos has its roots in the close cooperation and collective decision-making necessitated by wet-rice cultivation, which until recently was Japan's prime source of sustenance. The rice paddy, introduced to Japan in the late first millennium BCE, is labor-intensive: before mechanization, each rice plant had to be individually inserted into the ground. Even in modern times, household members subordinate their personal inclinations to work together for the good of the crop—and, by extension, for mutual survival. At a broader level, it is a village affair, in which a cluster of households assist one another in planting, weeding, and harvesting.

Such social cooperation and the absence of marked individualism have characterized Shinto from the outset. Over the centuries, the religion has always made a virtue of subordination to the well-being of the larger social unit, whether that unit be a household, a rice-growing village, a feudal domain, or the body of "salarymen" employed by a modern multinational corporation.

Despite the shadow of Japanese militarism and imperialism that fell across Shinto in the early post-war period, the religion continues to thrive and to command the affection, if not absolute loyalty, of the majority of the Japanese people. Indeed, in a great many respects, to be Japanese is to be Shinto, no matter what other religions one espouses.

CHAPTER ONE

ORIGINS AND HISTORICAL DEVELOPMENT

Shinto is deeply embedded in Japanese culture. For at least two thousand years—and perhaps far longer—it has commanded the devotion of the Japanese people, despite the introduction into the country of Buddhism, Confucianism, Daoism, and, more recently, Christianity. The evolution of Shinto can be traced from early archeological evidence (ca. 300BCE–300CE), through the Shinto revival in the eighteenth century and the period of "State Shinto" (1871–1945), to its current status in a country that is now a major economic power. In addition to noting how Buddhism and Shinto have complemented one another over the centuries, it is important to recognize the manner in which Shinto has absorbed elements of foreign religions while, at the same time, remaining distinctly Japanese.

LEFT: A pine tree atop a rock at Kiri-Kiri, Iwate. Such places of beauty have the powerful essence of natural kami *(spirits), which are central to Shinto belief.*

The origins of Shinto lie deep in the ancient past. It is open to question whether the prehistoric Jomon culture (ca. 11,000–300BCE) possessed a faith centered on the reverence of *kami* ("spirit," "deity," "divine being," or "god/goddess"; see pp.23–33), at least in anything like the form known today. These preliterate, seminomadic foragers and fisherfolk produced *dogu*, stylized female figurines with exaggerated hips and breasts. The precise nature of the beliefs surrounding *dogu* is unknown, although they probably reflect the existence of a fertility cult. *Dogu* were often placed in or near graves after being deliberately broken, perhaps ritually "killed," in order to release the spiritual "essence" of the *dogu*. But whether this "essence" was conceived in terms of anything resembling a prototypical Shinto *kami* remains entirely a matter of speculation.

However, strikingly Shintoistic iconographic evidence begins to appear with the arrival of the more complex Yayoi culture (ca. 300BCE–300CE). Among the grave goods associated with the Yayoi—rice cultivators whose homeland probably lay somewhere in southeastern Asia or southern China—are small ceramic images of grain storehouses that are remarkably similar to the architecture of the shrine at Ise, a form that has remained unaltered for at least twelve hundred years, although it is periodically rebuilt (see pp.62–3). Female fertility images also occur, as well as stone clubs that appear to have phallic symbolism. The introduction of rice-paddy agriculture seems to have brought with it rituals connected with sowing and harvesting that were probably fundamentally similar to rice-related Shinto rituals that persist to the present in rural Japan.

Closely associated with the Yayoi fertility cult are jewels called *magatama*, ceremonial mirrors, and sacred swords, all of which play a significant role in Shinto mythology (see p.29) and form part of the imperial regalia to this day. Many scholars suspect that the majority of the *ujigami*—the tutelary deities associated with the most ancient recorded Japanese *uji* ("clans")—date from this period. The most important *ujigami* was (and is) Amaterasu, the sun goddess (see pp.28–30)

Many scholars believe, that in the fourth century CE, Japan was conquered by horse-riding nomads from Central Asia—almost certainly a ruling élite rather than an invading population—and a new form of chieftain's tomb appeared: the *kofun*, or tumulus. Votive figurines of horses and warriors, known as *hanniwa*, were often placed around the periphery of these massive, keyhole-shaped mounds to accompany the deceased warlord on his journey to the afterworld.

A hanniwa *tomb figurine of a warrior—perhaps engaged in an act of devotion to a deity or lord—found at Yamato-mura in Ibaraki prefecture, eastern Honshu.*

By the early sixth century CE, the Yamato emperor exercised authority over most of the country to the south and west of the Kanto plain. It was to this embryonic state that the first substantial contingent of Buddhist missionaries traveled, in 552CE according to tradition, although scholars think 538CE more likely.

Many Yamato courtiers enthusiastically embraced Buddhism—albeit for the most part in a highly Shintoistic way, worshiping statues of the Buddha as manifestations of a powerful *kami*—while others resented its intrusion. However, in 592CE, the regent Prince Shotoku (Shotoku-Taishi) declared Buddhism the official religion of the imperial court. But most Japanese remained untouched by it until the early Heian era (794–1185CE). Buddhists did not attempt to undermine or supplant

Shinto, but simply founded their temples next to Shinto shrines and proclaimed that there was no fundamental conflict between the two faiths. Toward the end of the Heian era, this sense of inclusiveness led to the development of Ryobu Shinto, or "Double Shinto," in which Shinto *kami* and Buddhist *bosatsu* (*bodhisattva*s—an "enlightenment being" or *buddha*-to-be) were formally combined into single divine entities. This theological fusion was often visually represented by images of *kami* in human form "dreaming" of their *bosatsu* counterparts.

The last years of the Heian era were marked by a civil war that culminated in the appointment of Minamoto no Yoritomo to the new imperial office of shogun, or "generalissimo." Four centuries of almost constant internal strife followed. The most significant religious development of this period was the introduction of Christianity in 1549, but its initial gains were reversed following the assassination in 1582 of its early patron, the powerful *daimyo*, or warlord, Oda Nobunaga. Under the Tokugawa shogunate (1603–1867), Buddhism was in the ascendant, Chinese Neoconfucianism was also espoused, and Daoism came to occupy an important role.

However, in the late eighteenth century, the efforts of Motoori Norinaga (1730–1800) and other Shinto scholars led to a renewed interest in the *Kojiki*, the

Nihonshoki, and other ancient Shinto texts (see pp.37–45). A century later, this Shinto revival, which strongly emphasized the imperial cult, was a major factor in the collapse of the, by then, economically moribund shogunate and the restoration in 1868 of imperial power under Emperor Meiji. In the years immediately following the Meiji restoration, Shinto became the official religion of Japan (known as "State Shinto") and Buddhism went into a brief eclipse.

In the 1870s, Christian missionaries returned to a newly tolerant Japan, but few Japanese saw any merit in switching from Shinto, a faith closely associated with the imperial regime and hence also with the growing prosperity that was the result of the government's policy of Western-style industrialization. Today only around 600,000 Japanese profess the Christian faith (approximately half of them Roman Catholics).

In the late 1880s, the imperial government put an end to the backlash against Buddhism, and the Buddhist establishment made a rapid comeback. Shinto remained the state religion until 1945, but the historic balance between the two faiths was restored and persists to this day. "State Shinto" was disestablished after the end of the Second World War, and since then no faith has enjoyed official status.

Shinto, though, pervades Japanese life in many unexpected ways. For example, the national sport is sumo wrestling, which derives from an ancient Shinto ritual honoring the *kami*. The canopy over the ring is reminiscent of a Shinto shrine, the referee is dressed in garb similar to that of a Shinto priest, and the throwing of salt (thought to have magical properties) before a bout is believed to purify the ring. It is associations such as these that make the faith part of the social fabric.

An important phenomenon in the recent history of religion in Japan is the growth of the Shinko Shukyo ("New Religions"; see p.100), a term used to cover the new sects that began to arise in the early nineteenth century amid the social chaos that marked the collapse of shogun feudalism. For the most part, these sects were blends of Shinto and Buddhism, but since the Meiji restoration some have adopted elements of Christianity and other faiths. Many ceremonies and festivals are a blend of Shinto and Buddhism: for example, during Tokyo's annual Sanja festival, the *mikoshi* ("portable shrine") is carried through the grounds of the Asakusa temple and shrine. The Shinto shrine itself, which is adjacent to the Buddhist temple, is dedicated to three deified humans who had retrieved the Buddha image from the Sumida River and enshrined it.

A History of the Kingdom of Wei, ca. 297CE

“The people of Wa {Japan} dwell in the middle of the ocean on the mountainous islands southeast of [the prefecture of] Tai-fang. They formerly comprised more than one hundred communities. During the Han dynasty, [Wa] envoys appeared at the court; today, thirty of their communities maintain intercourse with us through envoys and scribes....

The land of Wa is warm and mild. In winter as in summer the people live on raw vegetables and go about barefooted. They have {or live in} houses; father and mother, elder and younger, sleep separately. They smear their bodies with pink and scarlet, just as the Chinese use powder. They serve food on bamboo and wooden trays, helping themselves with their fingers. When a person dies, they prepare a single coffin, without an outer one. They cover the graves with earth to make a mound. When death occurs, mourning is observed for more than ten days, during which period they do not eat meat. The head mourners wail and lament, while friends sing, dance, and drink liquor. When the funeral is over, all members of the family go into the water to cleanse themselves in a bath of purification.”

Tsunoda and Goodrich cited in *Sources of Japanese Tradition*, edited by Tsunoda, Rusaku., et al. Columbia University Press: New York, 1958, pp.6–7.

Commentary

Although there is some evidence of contact with China before ca. 250–60CE—in the form of inscriptions containing Chinese characters—the *Wei Chih* is the earliest account of Japan in a Chinese chronicle. It forms part of the history of the Kingdom of Wei (220–65CE), a successor state to the Han dynasty, which collapsed in 220CE. An embassy, composed primarily of merchants, visited what the Chinese called the "Kingdom of Wa" some time in the middle of the third century and returned with a detailed account of life in this "barbarian" neighbor that lay to the east of the Middle Kingdom. It was included, together with accounts of other barbarian realms on the fringe of China, when the official chronicle of the Kingdom of Wei was compiled ca. 297CE. The Chinese were intrigued by the fact that Wa had recently had a female ruler (Empress Pimiko) and that there were no horses there.

It also gives us our earliest glimpse of Shinto, especially as regards funeral practices. The construction of earthen mounds is reflected in the archeological record, while the account of the ten-day mourning period provides an insight into an important aspect of early Shinto that has all but disappeared since the advent of Buddhism in the sixth century CE (see p.16).

CHAPTER TWO

ASPECTS OF THE DIVINE

Shinto belief and practice revolve around the worship of supernatural beings known as *kami* who oversee all aspects of nature and human life. Such divine beings are believed to animate every object in the universe—from prominent geographical sites, such as Mount Fuji, to the souls of deceased children. The Shinto pantheon is said to contain an infinite number of *kami*—many of these are deities that have been incorporated from Buddhism and Daoism.

The oldest Japanese texts, the *Kojiki* and the *Nihonshoki* (see pp.37–9), tell how the world was created by the celestial deities Izanagi and Izanami. After what amounted to a false start, the primal pair gave birth to a host of *kami*, including the sovereign sun goddess Amaterasu, whose descendant, Jimmu Tenno, became the first emperor.

LEFT: Susano—the god of storms and brother of Amaterasu, the sun goddess—is one of Shinto's principal kami. *He is depicted in this late 19th-century hanging scroll slaying the eight-headed dragon Yamato no Orochi.*

The Shinto faith, like many of the world's major belief systems, conceives of a superior, or "divine," realm which informs and guides human existence. This realm is populated by a host of beings known as *kami*. Some aspects of the Shinto pantheon resemble the pantheons of other ancient religions, in the simple sense that gods and goddesses are venerated. However, other features of the Shinto divine are reminiscent of what in other belief systems are heroic rather than divine figures: a great many *kami* are far more "human" than the gods and goddesses of other religions and, in some cases, take human form.

The Japanese word *kami* is often translated as "deity," but in fact it designates an extremely wide range of spirit-beings together with a host of mysterious and supernatural forces and "essences." In the *Kojiki* (see p.38), it is said that there are eight million *kami* (in Japanese mythology, eight is a sacred number that means simply "many", and thus expresses infinite). These include countless vaguely defined tutelary divinities of clans, villages, and neighborhoods (*ujigami*); "spirits of place"—the essences of prominent geographical features, including mountains, rivers, and waterfalls; and other natural phenomena, such as the *kamikaze* ("divine wind"), the typhoon that saved Japan from a seaborne Mongol invasion in the thirteenth century.

Many *kami* live in the sky and come down to Earth periodically to visit sacred places and shrines. They are considered so sacred that worshipers must purify themselves before entering shrine precincts or taking part in festivals (see pp.81–4) that are held in their honor.

Some *kami* are benign imported Buddhist and Daoist deities; others are demonic, vengeful spirits who are responsible for a wide variety of mortal troubles. In Japanese tradition, most evil spirits or *oni* ("demons") are invisible, although some are claimed to be giants, of various colors, with horns and sometimes three eyes. Others, however, are thought to be animal spirits who have the capacity to possess a person—in such cases, they must be exorcised by a priest. Among the most feared is the fox spirit—possession by this being can bring about all sorts of calamities, including illness and death. In parts of rural Japan, especially in the north, where old customs and beliefs often linger, the *yamabushi* ("mountain warriors"; see p.75, are considered particularly adept at exorcising such spirits and thereby restoring the victim to good health.

Another variety of evil spirit is the *obake*, or ghost. These entities are also believed to be capable of causing considerable harm, but they can be driven off with appropriately respectful rituals (see pp.92–3).

Worshipers parade with a mikoshi *("portable shrine") in front of the spectacular waterfall in Akita, northwestern Honshu, which is thought to be favored by the local* kami.

The Shinto tradition does not believe that there is an absolute dichotomy of good and evil. Rather, all phenomena, both animate and inanimate, are thought to possess both "rough" and "gentle," or negative and positive, characteristics and it is possible for a given entity to manifest either of these characteristics depending on the circumstances. Thus, in spite of their malevolence, *oni* are somewhat ambivalent characters. For example, the malicious fox spirit is also closely associated with Inari, the rice god, who is an extremely popular and charitable *kami* (see p.30). Similarly, the grotesque bird-man figures called *tengu* can also be the benevolent guardians of *kami*, and for this reason they are often impersonated at Shinto festivals. Another example of this ambivalence is Susano, who, after his banishment from heaven, became a positive figure, slaying a dragon and saving a maiden in distress (see p.29). In all cases, the misfortunes inflicted by *oni* are seen as the result of a temporary disruption of the natural order of things, and not the manifestation of an inherent evil force.

Ancestral spirits form another important category of *kami*. In Shinto, a person's soul is believed to become a *kami* after the death of its mortal "host," and the *kami* of a family's ancestors are revered at household shrines. Some ancestral *kami*, such as the spirits of Emperor Meiji (reigned 1867–1912) and other rulers, may become the focus of more widespread cults. For example, Meiji's shrine is the most important Shinto shrine in Tokyo. The *kami* of all Japan's war dead since 1872 are worshiped at Tokyo's controversial Yasukuni shrine (see pp.99–100).

The most widely known *kami* are the anthropomorphic gods and goddesses who emerged during what ancient texts call the "Age of the Gods." Accounts of this primeval era—when deities were active on Earth before establishing the rule of their mortal descendants, the emperors, and then withdrawing to the heavenly domain—are given in the epics the *Kojiki* (712CE) and the *Nihonshoki* (720CE), together with the stories of the great gods and goddesses of Shinto (see pp.37–43).

The greatest of these divine offspring of Izanagi and Izanami was the venerated sun goddess, Amaterasu (the "Person Who Makes the Heavens Shine"), chief of the pantheon and the most important Shinto divinity. After she had established her sovereignty, following an argument with her brother Susano (see pp.42–3), she established the imperial line through her descendant Jimmu Tenno, who became Japan's first emperor.

The *kami* in the "Age of the Gods" are the *amatsukami* ("heavenly *kami*") and the *kunitsukami* ("earthly *kami*"). Amaterasu is one of the former, while the popular Okuninushi, the guardian god of Japan and its emperors, is one of the latter. The story of the establishment of the rule of Jimmu Tenno and the Japanese imperial line is an important part of Shinto belief and is closely associated with the Yamato region of Honshu, the main island and the area where Shinto's most important shrine is located: that of Amaterasu at Ise (see p.62).

After Susano's descent to the "Reed Plain" (Earth), he saved a beautiful maiden from a hideous dragon, found a fabulous sword in one of its eight tails, and gave it to his sister, Amaterasu, as a peace offering. He married the maiden, built a palace near Izumo, and fathered a dynasty of powerful deities who came to rule the Earth. The greatest of them was Okuninushi, the "Great Lord of the Country." Alarmed at Okuninushi's power, Amaterasu sent her grandson Honinigi to the mortal world to reestablish her sovereignty over the Earth.

Honinigi bore three talismans of sovereignty—a sacred mirror, which had been used to trick Amaterasu into returning after an argument with Susano (see p.42); a magical sword, later called Kusanagi, which Susano had discovered in the dragon's tail; and a wondrous fertility jewel called a *magatama*, which Susano had used to produce offspring in the contest with his sister (see p.42).

According to tradition, Honinigi landed at Mount Takachio, in Kyushu, and struck a deal with Okuninushi. In return for the latter's loyalty, Honinigi promised that his grandmother would recognize Okuninushi as the perpetual protector of the imperial family, which was later founded by Honinigi's great-grandson, the aforementioned Jimmu Tenno. Okuninushi is enshrined at Izumo-*taisha*, the second most important Shinto shrine in Japan (after Ise), and since the days of Jimmu Tenno the earthly descendants of Amaterasu have ruled Japan as emperors.

Another prominent *kami* is Inari, the rice god, who is widely venerated as the deity who ensures an abundant rice harvest and, by extension, general prosperity throughout the land—thus he is especially important to shopkeepers, merchants, and artisans. Inari's messenger and guardian is the fox, and images of this wily animal are prominent at all the god's shrines (see p.66).

There are also the so-called *Shichifukujin* ("Seven Lucky Gods"), each of whom personifies a desirable characteristic or condition. The most popular of the septet are Daikokuten and Ebisu, who are often enshrined together and are sometimes said to be father and son. Both personify wealth and material abundance. Daikokuten, typically depicted with a large sack slung over his left shoulder, is a tutelary god of the kitchen and is particularly revered by cooks and restaurateurs. He is frequently assimilated to Okuninushi (see p.29), who is also known as Daikokusama. Ebisu carries a fishing rod in one hand and a sea bream under his other arm. The other five are Benten (god of skill in music and other arts), Fukurokuju (god of popularity), Hotei (god of contentment and magnanimity), Jurojin (god of longevity), and, finally, Bishamonten (god of benevolent authority).

In Japanese Buddhism a similarly broad array of sacred beings, known as *butsu* and *bosatsu* ("enlightened being") are venerated. Three of these divine beings loom especially large—Amida, Kannon, and Jizo. Amida presides over the "Pure Land," or Western Paradise; Kannon is the protector of children, dead souls, and women in childbirth; it is also the *bosatsu* to whom worshipers turn for mercy and forgiveness; and the *bosatsu* Jizo is also concerned with children, particularly with the souls of those who have died (including, in recent times, aborted fetuses). Jizo is the protector of all who suffer pain. Kannon and Jizo are also worshiped as *kami* by vast numbers of Japanese. In fact, in popular worship, the distinction between Shinto *kami* and Buddhist *bosatsu* and *butsu* is very blurred. At times in the past, Shinto priests have used the phrase "*kami*-nature" in a fashion analogous to the Buddhist term "*buddha*-nature," which is a reference to our true nature or essence.

Both *kami* and *bosatsu* are seen as essentially complementary, and a number of divinities are important to both faiths, such as Hachiman, an important warrior-god largely derived from the semilegendary emperor

Ojin (ca. 300CE). Hachiman is widely worshiped throughout Japan at both Buddhist temples and Shinto shrines. Most notably, he is the tutelary deity of the Todaiji temple in Nara (which also houses the largest statue of the Buddha in Japan) and of the Hachiman shrine in Kamakura.

Hachiman shrines are favorite venues for the ritual called *omiyamairi* in which infants—primarily boys in the case of Hachiman—are taken to shrines for the first time and purified (see p.85). At the same time, Hachiman's image is to be found in a great many Buddhist temples, where he is venerated as a *bosatsu*.

Hachiman is not the only deity with historical or quasihistorical roots. Possibly the best example of all is Sugawara no Michizane, otherwise known as Tenjin, or "Heaven Person." A brilliant administrator and scholar, Sugawara (845–903CE) was at the peak of his career as a member of the Heian court when several jealous colleagues conspired against him. Falsely accused of misconduct in office, Sugawara was banished from his native city and spent the rest of his life as a restless political exile on the island of Kyushu, where he eventually died an unhappy death. After his demise, Heian, the imperial capital (modern-day Kyoto), was devastated by fires and pestilence. The imperial authorities were convinced that this was divine retribution for their treatment of Sugawara no Michizane and they sought to appease his angry spirit and placate his ghost by building a major shrine to the dead scholar as a *kami* under the name Tenjin—the magnificent Kitano Temmangu shrine, which remains one of the most important Shinto shrines in modern Kyoto.

According to the story, conditions in Heian immediately improved. Thereafter, Tenjin became an important member of the Shinto pantheon, venerated throughout Japan as the patron of learning and scholarship—his cult spread the length and breadth of the country. Tenjin shrines are visited regularly by students (and their parents), who want to invoke the *kami*'s assistance prior to the taking of important examinations, and by scholars who are seeking divine help in their research.

New additions are frequently made to the roster of major *kami*. For example, the spirit of Emperor Meiji, during whose reign (1867–1912) Japan moved from being a backward East Asian country to the status of a world power, is venerated in the largest shrine in Tokyo, the Meiji-*jingu*; and the spirit of Ieyasu, the first Tokugawa shogun (died 1616), is magnificently enshrined at Nikko. This ability to grow and change with the times is part of the essential genius of Shinto.

Japan: The Land of the Gods

"People all over the world refer to Japan as the Land of the Gods and call us the descendants of the gods. Indeed, it is exactly as they say: our country, as a special mark of favor from the heavenly gods, was begotten by them, and there is thus so immense a difference between Japan and all the other countries of the world as to defy comparison. Ours is a splendid and blessed country, the Land of the Gods beyond any doubt, and we, down to the most humble man and woman, are the descendants of the gods. Nevertheless, there are unhappily many people who do not understand why Japan is the Land of the Gods and we their descendants....

Is this not a lamentable state of affairs? Japanese differ completely from and are superior to the peoples of China, India, Russia, Holland, Siam, Cambodia, and all other countries of the world, and for us to have called our country the Land of the Gods was not mere vainglory. It was the gods who formed all the lands of the world at the Creation, and these gods were without exception born in Japan. Japan is thus the homeland of the gods, and that is why we call it the Land of the Gods."

From *Kodo Taii* in *Hirata Atsutane Zenshu I*, pp.22–3, cited in *Sources of Japanese Tradition*, edited by Tsunoda, Rusaku., et al. Columbia University Press: New York, 1958, p.544.

Commentary

Hirata Atsutane (1776–1843) was a disciple of the great Shinto scholar Motoori Norinaga (see pp.49–50) who carried on the latter's ground-breaking research and textual criticism. In the passage cited he explains why Japan is the "Land of the Gods." Despite Japan's deliberate political isolation from the rest of the world during the Tokugawa shogunate (1603–1867), memories of the so-called "Christian century" (ca. 1550–1650) lingered on, and Western ideas continued to trickle into Japan via the Dutch presence in Nagasaki.

Drawing on his knowledge of both Chinese and Western religious ideas, Hirata concluded that it was Shinto and its pantheon of divine figures that set Japan apart from other nations. In his opinion, the Japanese people were ultimately descended from the *kami* who populate the *Kojiki* and the *Nihonshoki* (also called the *Nihongi)* and they were therefore superior to other races. Indeed, as he saw it, unlike other countries with which he was familiar, Japan was the homeland of the gods and therefore especially blessed. Like those of his mentor Motoori, Hirata's writings fueled the later stages of the Shinto Revival (1770s–1870s) and helped to lay the foundation for the emergence of "State Shinto" in the wake of the Meiji restoration in 1868.

CHAPTER THREE

SACRED TEXTS

The most important written sources for Shinto are the *Kojiki* and *Nihonshoki*, which were composed, respectively, in 712CE by the Heian courtier Ono Yasumaro and in 720CE by a committee of scholars, who sought to rectify what they believed to be Ono's excessive emphasis on the imperial, or Yamato, clan.

Unlike the Western "scriptures"—divinely revealed (or dictated) messages—these works are genealogically based chronicles that record both the divine and human generations that have unfolded since the "Age of the Gods" (see p.28) and the creation of the world. Both texts undoubtedly owe a debt to the ancient Chinese tradition (the *Nihonshoki* is written in classical Chinese) which had such a dramatic impact on Japanese culture and belief in the eighth century CE.

LEFT: A Shinto priest intones prayers as part of the annual Saigusa Matsuri (Lily Festival) at the Isagawa shrine in Nara.

The *Kojiki* ("Record of Ancient Matters"), the oldest surviving text in Japanese, was compiled and edited in 712CE by the scholar-courtier Ono Yasumaro from a number of earlier sources. These sources, some written (and since lost) and others oral, were for the most part genealogies of the several powerful *uji* ("clans"), that dominated Japanese political life in the Nara period (710–94CE), the most important being the imperial Yamato clan. Each genealogy traced the descent of the *uji* in question back to a particular *kami* ("spirit"; see p.24).

At this period, Japan was actively borrowing almost every conceivable cultural trait from China. Inspired by the Chinese genre of "imperial chronicle," which served to legitimize the ruling dynasty, the Japanese court commissioned Ono to compile a coherent Japanese chronicle that would establish for all time the supremacy of the Yamato clan. The early part of Ono's text contains the primary account of Shinto cosmology and theogony: the creation of the islands of Japan by the primordial deities Izanagi and Izanami; the birth of the sun goddess Amaterasu; the extension of her authority to the "Reed Plain" (Earth); and the appearance of her descendant Jimmu Tenno, the first emperor (see pp.28–30).

The leading Japanese clans were apparently dissatisfied with the *Kojiki* even before Ono had completed it, largely because it emphasized the history of the imperial clan at the expense of their own. The court acted on the dissatisfaction the clans expressed by commissioning the *Nihonshoki* ("Chronicles of Japan"), also known as the *Nihongi*, from a committee of courtiers.

Ono had produced a relatively straightforward narrative, but the authors of the *Nihonshoki* felt compelled to retell each important mythological event from a variety of perspectives, reflecting the versions sacred to the several major clans. The result was a jumble of compromises, redundancies, and even contradictions. Nonetheless, the *Nihonshoki*, compiled in 720CE, is a treasure trove of tales that shed a great deal of light on the range and diversity of ancient Shinto mythology and its *kami*.

Unlike the *Kojiki*, the *Nihonshoki* is written in classical Chinese, although it includes poetic sections in archaic Japanese. Wherever possible, the authors presented the myths from a Chinese perspective, and the text contains a great many Chinese mythological themes and references—a good example is the Pan Gu story, a Chinese creation myth that recurs in almost identical form at several points in the *Nihonshoki*.

Both the *Kojiki* and the *Nihonshoki* state that in the beginning, when the world was a fluid, turbulent,

formless chaos, there arose seven successive generations of invisible *kami*. In the eighth generation, the heavenly divinity Izanagi (the "August Male") and his sister the goddess Izanami (the "August Female") came into being and, standing on the "Floating Bridge of Heaven" (probably to be interpreted as a rainbow), they dipped a jeweled spear into the jelly-like mass and created an island, Onogoro. This was the first land. Izanagi and Izanami descended to the island. At this point they became aware of their gender difference and had sexual intercourse. But Izanami's first offspring was a "leech-

Omamori *are sacred talismans used to contain prayers and invocations that ensure the wearer's general good fortune.*

child" (that is, a monster), and the couple sought help from the older *kami*. Izanami then gave birth to an array of *kami* and also islands—the Japanese archipelago. But the birth of her last child, the fire god, caused her such severe burns that she died and went to Yomi, the land of the dead (see pp.94–5).

Izanagi ventured into Yomi in an attempt to retrieve his beloved wife, but, like the Greek Orpheus in his attempt to rescue his beloved Eurydice from Hades, Izanagi disregarded her plea not to look upon her. He saw that Izanami had become a rotting, hideous demon, and fled in horror, pursued by Izanami and the so-called "Hags of Yomi." His effort was unsuccessful, and he barely escaped with his life.

To purify himself of Yomi's pollution, Izanagi bathed in the sacred Hi River. As he washed, the sun goddess

Amaterasu was born from his left eye, the moon god Tsukiyomi from his right eye, and the storm god Susano (also known as the "Raging Male") from his nose. Izanagi then retired to the northwest part of Kyushu island, where today there are a handful of shrines dedicated to him and Izanami. Before retiring, Izanagi handed power to his offspring: Amaterasu (the "Person Who Makes the Heavens Shine") was to be supreme deity, Tsukiyomi became lord of the night (the moon god), and Susano was given dominion of the sea.

However, Susano was jealous of his sister and challenged her authority. After claiming victory in a divinatory contest, wherein he and his divine sister vied to see who could produce the greater number of offspring (Susano produced more, but Amaterasu's brood included a greater number of males), Susano rampaged through heaven, causing chaos. Amaterasu's response was to shut herself away in the "Heavenly Cave of Darkness," which made matters worse by depriving the world of sunlight and causing the crops to wither. Using a reflective mirror to entice her, the gods eventually tricked Amaterasu into reappearing and, as she did so, the sunlight returned. Susano was then banished from heaven—descending to Earth in Izumo near the headwaters of the Hi River—and the sun goddess's sovereignty was confirmed. Her descendant Jimmu Tenno became the first emperor, and with the establishment of the imperial line, the "Age of the Gods"came to an end.

The *Kojiki* and *Nihonshoki* are by no means the only sources of Shinto beliefs. Other writings include the *Manyoshu* ("Collection of 10,000 Leaves," ca. 760CE), a vast anthology of poetry that embraces poems on religious, mythological, and secular themes. This is considered the single greatest piece of literature dating from the Nara period and is best known, not for its thousands of examples of classic Japanese verse known as *tanka*s, but for the very long poems called *choka* which provide a means of dealing with important subjects, such as the imperial family.

In addition, there are the *Fudoki*—provincial chronicles commissioned in 713CE that include legends of local *kami*—and the literature on the laws of Shinto contained in a large body of books, some fifty in total, known as the *Engishiki*. This collection dates from the late tenth century CE—it is named for the Engi era (901–22CE)—and includes a vast anthology of *norito* (Shinto ritual prayers and liturgies for use in public ceremonies), as well as instructions on how to apply the *jingi-ryo*—rules that must be adhered to when conducting Shinto and shrine ceremonies.

Japan's Creation in the *Kojiki* and the *Nihonshoki*

“At this time the heavenly deities, all with one command, said to the two deities Izanagi-nö-mikötö and Izanami-nö-mikötö: ‘Complete and solidify this drifting land!’
Giving them the Heavenly Jeweled Spear, they entrusted the mission to them.
Thereupon, the two deities stood on the Heavenly Floating Bridge and, lowering the jeweled spear, stirred with it. They stirred the brine with a churning-churning sound; and when they lifted up [the spear] again, the brine dripping down from the tip of the spear piled up and became an island. This was the island Onögörö. [*Kojiki*]”

“Izanagi no Mikoto and Izanami no Mikoto stood on the floating bridge of Heaven, and held counsel together, saying: ‘Is there not a country beneath?’ Thereupon they thrust down the jewel-spear of Heaven, and groping about therewith found the ocean. The brine dripped from the point of the spear coagulated and became an island which received the name of Ono-goro-jima. [*Nihonshoki*]”

From *Kojiki*, translated by Donald L. Philippi. Princeton University Press: Princeton, 1969, p.49 and *Nihongi, Chronicles of Japan from the Earliest Times to A.D. 697. Vol 1*, translated by W.G. Aston. Kegan Paul, Trench, Trübner & Co. Limited: London, 1896, pp.10–12.

Commentary

The narratives contained in the *Kojiki* and *Nihonshoki*, especially in the early sections thereof, are the closest approximation in Shinto of "scriptural" texts. Izanagi and Izanami (see p.40) have been called the "Japanese Adam and Eve," and their role in Japan's mythology is essentially similar to that of the Old Testament pair—although in a number of important respects it is much more extensive, because they not only procreate divine beings but also bring into existence a long list of islands and other inanimate phenomena.

The passages opposite—the same episode as it is described in the *Kojiki* and then the *Nihonshoki*—relate to the couple's creation of the primordial Japanese island, Onogoro (see p.40). Like a great many other creation stories, these versions assume that the primeval state of things is one of flux and that form needs to be given where none exists (a similar example of this is the ancient Greek concept of *chaos*, a "void" out of which order was brought forth). Thus, the Japanese divine pair is charged by the heavenly divinities with congealing this amorphous, gel-like substance into a solid mass. This they do with a "jeweled spear"—symbolic, perhaps, of the male reproductive organ. Thus is the ordered, Japanese "cosmos" created from primeval chaos.

鸕鷀草葺不合尊第四の子御諱を神日本磐余彦
と申し天照太神より五代の孫日向國宮崎に都を
天皇御年四十五諸皇子と師を率ひて安藝に
到り吉備を經攝津河内を殉給ふに長髄
彦を討ち給ふを天照太神の夢想に因て頭八
咫烏を郷導として菟田に出で兄猾を討ち八十
梟を討ち兄磯城を討ち六年にして中州
定まり大和國畝傍山の東南橿
原に都し正月天皇位に即給ひ歳を改めて
元年とす七十六年三月崩ぜ寿一百廿一歳
傍山の東北の陵に葬る是を人皇の始めと爲るなり
大蘇芳年

CHAPTER FOUR

SACRED PERSONS

Every major religion recognizes the special significance of one or more individuals to its tradition, whether they be embodiments of the godhead, founder figures, scholars, teachers, saints, mystics, or guides. Although Shinto has no known founder, there are several individuals whose lives and ideas are deeply embedded in the tradition—figures such as Ono Yasumaro, who compiled the *Kokiji*; Motoori Norinaga, the great eighteenth-century Shinto scholar; Miki Nakayama, the founder of Tenrikyo; as well as the many Buddhists, including Honen and Nichiren, whose influence on the faith has been profound. Equally significant is the figure of the emperor who, after 1868, was established as the incarnation of Japanese nationhood and was believed to be a direct descendant of Shinto's principal deity, Amaterasu.

LEFT: Jimmu Tenno, Japan's legendary first emperor and descendant of the sun goddess Amaterasu. He is depicted in this 19th-century print delivering his people to their new homeland with the help of his divine crow.

In the last two thousand years, great contributions have been made to Japan's religious development by a wide range of individuals—from priests and monks to bureaucrats, princes, and emperors. Among these were the mainstream Buddhist, Honen (1133–1212) and the quarrelsome, charismatic, fanatical, and ultra-patriotic Buddhist, Nichiren (1222–82), who cut against the Japanese grain and whose teachings remained relatively insignificant until the twentieth century, when an organization called the Soka Gakkai (the "Value-Creating Society") launched a campaign to revive them. Since the Second World War, Soka Gakkai and Nichiren-shoshu (a sect based on Nichiren's teachings) have gained millions of supporters, but remain controversial among mainstream Shintoists and Buddhists.

Of the many Shinto and Buddhist thinkers and scholars who have appeared in Japan in the centuries since, none—including the great eighteenth-century Shinto scholar Motoori Norinaga—rivals the stature of the galaxy of seminal figures who emerged in the lifetimes of Honen and Nichiren. Between them, they established the religious framework that still governs Japanese Buddhism and that has also had a profound impact on the evolution of Shinto, as the two faiths have sought to find common ground.

Those who have featured prominently in the history of Shinto include scholars who have striven tirelessly to preserve the ancient stories of the *kami* faith. Prominent among them are Ono Yasumaro, compiler of the *Kojiki*, and, a millennium later, Motoori Norinaga (1730–1800C, who was probably the greatest of all Shinto scholars. Motoori was largely responsible for bringing about the Shinto revival known as Kokugaku ("National Learning Movement") from the late 1700s. He studied medicine before devoting himself to the study of Japanese mythological classics, especially the *Kojiki* and the *Nihonshoki* (see pp.38–43). He was inspired by the Shingon Buddhist monk Keichu (1640–1701) and, more immediately, by Kamo no Mabuchi (1697–1769). Both had sought to define Japanese national identity with reference to the ancient Shinto texts.

After his medical studies, Motoori spent his life interpreting the *kami* faith and attracted a wide following. His masterpiece, the monumental, forty-four-volume *Kojiki den* ("Interpretation of the *Kojiki*," 1798) is both an exhaustive exegesis of the *Kojiki* and a vast compendium of knowledge about ancient Japan. Motoori came to believe that Chinese influence—including Buddhism—had long obscured the essential Japanese character. Neither Motoori nor his two intellectual predecessors explicitly renounced Buddhism, but their attitude toward it was generally negative. Motoori attacked Buddhists and Confucian scholars for seeking to "know the unknowable."

Anti-Chinese sentiment and the importance of the Shinto *kami*—two themes that Motoori promoted tirelessly—were significant elements in Kokugaku and had a profound influence on the men who engineered the Meiji restoration in 1868. By the end of the Meiji era in 1912, thirteen Shinto-based sects were recognized by the Japanese government (see p.102). One of these was the Tenrikyo ("Heavenly Truth") sect. It was founded in 1838 by a farmer's wife named Miki Nakayama (1798–1887), who lived near the ancient capital, Nara. One night, while caring for her sick son, she went into a trance and was possessed by a *kami* who identified himself as Tentaishogun, the "Great Heavenly Generalissimo." In a series of possessions, Tentaishogun revealed that he and his nine subordinate entities were the only true *kami*, and that they had chosen Miki to spread their message. This message was eventually set down in a 1,711-verse poem called the *Ofudesaki* (literally, "The Tip of the Divine Writing Brush"). Completed in 1883, after fifteen years of work, the poem contains the revelations that Miki received concerning the nature of heaven, the *kami* who dwell there, and the role of humankind in the divine scheme of things—a role which is analogous to that played by a child with regard to his or her parents. Thus, the prime manifestation of the godhead in the Tenrikyo faith is called the Oyakami, "God the Parent."

In time, Tenrikyo developed into a major Shinto sect and is one of the most successful of Japan's "New Religions" (see pp.100–103). Although its concern with the afterlife reflects some features of the Buddhist "Pure Land" theology, its core doctrine stems directly from the fundamental Shinto concept of *kami*, and the idea that the universe and all that it contains are animated by a hierarchy of deities (see pp.24–5).

For much of Japanese history, the nominal head of the country has been just that—a ruler in name only, conducting rites for the nation as a sort of high priest of Shintoism but exercising little, if any, real power. The advent of "State Shinto" in 1872 was intimately linked with the cult of the emperor and beneath the whole elaborate structure of emperor-worship lay an infrastructure of myth that had its roots in the *Kojiki* (see p.38).

Under the Meiji reforms, the emperor continued to have little to do with the day-to-day business of government, but he became the focus of an intense cult as

A 19th-century triptych showing the sun goddess Amaterasu, whose return to the world is greeted with joy by the other gods.

the living incarnation of Japanese nationhood. After 1868, the divinity of the emperor—previously accepted in an abstract way—became a central tenet of state ideology. Children were taught in school that he was a direct descendant of Amaterasu, the sun goddess; they learned, too, that the nation's history began in 660BCE with the legendary emperor Jimmu Tenno, the great-great-great-grandson of this principal deity.

While most patriotic Japanese were happy to accept this version of events, extreme nationalists went further, claiming that the divine descent made the Japanese distinct from all other peoples—they were the "children of the gods." In the 1930s, such claims were to be used to justify imperialism on the grounds that foreign nationals were intrinsically inferior (see p.34). Indeed, it was not until the imposition by the occupying powers of the post-war constitution in 1947 that the emperor renounced his divinity—reigning henceforth not as a god but a constitutional monarch, or, more specifically, as the "symbol" rather than the "head" of state—and Japan firmly separated religion and the state.

Since the war, the importance of the emperor as the repository of peaceful desires has been stressed. An article of the Constitution of the Association of Shinto Shrines in 1956 stressed: "In accordance with the emperor's will, let us be harmonious and peaceful, and pray for the nation's development as well as the world's co-prosperity."

To this day, the imperial rituals, including enthronement, marriage, the symbolic planting of rice in the imperial palace paddy, and the emperor's annual visit to the Meiji shrine to pay homage to his ancestor, are all Shinto based. Although the post-war constitution stipulates that they are the private religious practices of the family, it is clear that many Japanese still regard them as having significance for the well-being of the nation.

The Supremacy of the Sun Goddess

“That the Sun Goddess is the sun in heaven is clear from the records of the *Kojiki* and the *Nihongi* [*Nihonshoki*]. If it is so beyond any doubt, is not the person who raises an objection the one who is obstinate? This Sun Goddess casts her light to the very extremities of the universe, but in the beginning it was in our Imperial Land that she made her appearance, and as the sovereign of the Imperial Line, that is, of the Imperial Land, she has reigned supreme over the Four Seas until now. When this Goddess hid herself in a cave in heaven, closing its doors, darkness fell over the countries of the world. You ask why darkness did not reign everywhere before her birth, a question a child might well ask. It seems childish indeed when a question which might spring from the doubts of a child is asked with such insistence by you. But this very point proves that the ancient happenings of the Divine Age are the facts and not fabrications. Some say that the records are the fabrication of later sovereigns, but who would fabricate such shallow sounding, incredible things? This is a point you should reflect upon seriously.”

Cited in *Sources of Japanese Tradition*, edited by Tsunoda, Rusaku., et al. Columbia University Press: New York, 1958, p.524.

Commentary

In the extract opposite, Motoori Norinaga—perhaps the most important Shinto theologian, who, almost single-handedly, brought about the Shinto revival in the late eighteenth-century—is responding to an objection that Amaterasu cannot be the sun, because the sun was present before the goddess's birth. In so doing, Motoori is attacking the Confucianist assumption that there is inevitably a rationalist solution to every problem. He counters by pointing out that the goddess "casts her light to the very extremities of the universe," and that when she withdrew into a cave (known as Ama-no-Iwato, or the "Heavenly Cave of Darkness," and said to have been in the vicinity of Ise) in response to Susano's rampage through heaven (see p.42), the world was plunged into a terrifying and life-threatening darkness.

Motoori goes on to assert that there must have been light before Amaterasu was born, but that once she was present she came to embody the sun as the prime source of light and its life-giving energy. Confucian rationalism, he concludes, is not sufficient to explain the "real" events that occurred during the "Age of the Gods." Indeed, Motoori argues that because no one would fabricate such an account, therefore the events must be true.

CHAPTER FIVE

ETHICAL PRINCIPLES

One of the most important ancient ethical codes informing Japanese belief and behavior is the prioritization of group solidarity over individual identity. Although to some extent inherited from Chinese culture, this code is powerfully reinforced by Shinto's long-standing emphasis upon the veneration of ancestral spirits, and family, and clan, solidarity.

Of equal significance is the tradition's concentration upon personal and ritual purity, and reverence for nature—all of which are basic tenets of the faith. Such principles have profoundly influenced Japanese behavior, from prehistoric times onward, and have played important roles in the modern Japanese environmental movement—those people caring for local Shinto shrines have often been at the forefront of efforts to clean up the countryside.

LEFT: A young boy petitioner respectfully lights a candle at a shrine to Inari. Characteristic torii *("sacred gateways") can be seen in the background.*

It is sometimes claimed that the Japanese rely solely on their Buddhist heritage for ethical guidance. However, this does not stand up to scrutiny. At the core of Shinto theology lies the idea that *wa* ("benign harmony") is inherent in nature and human relationships, and that anything that disrupts this state is bad. This helps to explain the widespread and deeply rooted Japanese belief that the individual is less important than the group, be it family, school, or workplace. Rules governing human behavior are considered necessary for the maintenance of *wa*, without which both society and the natural world would disintegrate into chaos. This ancient Chinese concept has guided both Japanese Shinto and Buddhist behavior for more than fifteen hundred years.

Confucian and Daoist ideas imported from China also claimed that chaos would follow if social nonconformity was tolerated, but these concepts served principally to reinforce the existing Shinto ethic, which sprang from the clan-based society of prehistoric and ancient Japan. This ethic revolves around two fundamental and intimately related concepts: the need to maintain the *tatemae* ("face") that a person presents to the outside world; and the *ie* ("extended household"), which includes all the ancestral spirits (see pp.90–91). The idea that Japanese ethics are based on shame rather than guilt has been exaggerated, but it is nonetheless true that conformity is enforced to a large degree by the loss of *tatemae* that an individual—and consequently his or her *ie*, school, employer, or other social group—would suffer as a result of violating part of the social code. Depending on the seriousness of the loss of face, a person may atone by bowing deeply, by a ceremonial act of gift-giving, or by committing suicide. Even today, suicide is often blamed on a person's inability to cope with the shame of, say, failing an examination.

If a whole group is stigmatized, a collective act of atonement is made. For example, when Japan's famous Shinkansen "Bullet Train" is late, every employee from the engineer to the conductor, hostesses, and ticket sellers feels responsible and will apologize profusely to delayed passengers. Once atonement is made, the shame ceases and the burden it imposes is lifted.

The Shinto ethic reached its apogee during the "State Shinto" era (1872–1945), when obedience to the emperor became the noblest form of behavior—up to and including sacrificing one's life for his benefit. It is very much a "this-worldly" phenomenon, with little or no emphasis placed on reward or punishment in the afterlife (see pp.90–93). However, the state of the soul after death is very much the concern of Japan's Buddhist traditions. From the outset, Mahayana Buddhism has had a well-defined concept of inherent human wickedness, and the Buddhist's ultimate goal is to achieve salvation in the form of *nirvana*, or release from the cycle of birth, death, and rebirth. This cycle is fueled by the accumulation of merit and demerit, a concept known as *karma*. In the Buddhist view, demerit springs from

Purification rituals at Japanese shrines and temples involve cleaning the hands and mouth with fresh water.

desire, and the loss of desire is thus the key to salvation. In Japan, this deep-rooted Buddhist insistence on suppressing personal desire complements the Shinto ethical tradition that demands subordination to the group in such a way that *wa* is nourished and maintained.

Anything that contributes to *wa* is, by definition, good; those things—behavior, emotions, desire, and so on—that disrupt it are perceived as being fundamentally evil. This belief also applies to humankind's relationship with nature and underscores the pervasive Shinto concern with maintaining a balance between the human and natural realms. Indeed, those individuals associated with local Shinto shrines have often taken the lead in campaigns to clean up rivers and lakes.

The Shinto obsession with *wa* is also reflected in a variety of Japanese customs that, at first glance, might not seem religious, such as removing one's shoes before entering a house and taking a daily bath (known as *ofuro*). Both customs are, essentially, expressions not only of purification—the interior of a home is, after all, a "sacred space" compared to the outside world—but also of the maintenance of a harmonious balance in the world.

Renewal and purification are, then, persistent themes of Shinto practice and belief. Every shrine has a trough containing pure water for the ritual ablutions—rinsing of the hands and mouth—required before one approaches the image of the *kami*. The worshiper scoops out some water with a bamboo dipper, pours it over his or her hands, and lightly rinses the mouth, thereby purifying the body both inside and out, and making it fit to enter the presence of the gods. The human body is thus cleansed and its internal balance is restored through acts of ritual purification such as these, which are known as *oharai*. A similar ritual is undertaken by *miko* girls ("shrine virgins") when they perform a dance known as a *kagura*, which is a celebration of the renewal of life.

Other important purification and renewal practices include the annual replacement of miniature family shrines and the periodic rebuilding of major shrines in order to invest them with life and vigor. All the buildings in Shinto's most sacred and revered shrine complex, Ise (see p.69)—near the coast southeast of Nara in Mie prefecture—have, since the eighth century CE, been replaced every twenty years by replicas that are exact copies down to the last wooden peg (the most recent rebuilding occurred in 1993). The symbolism here is extremely important: with each rebuilding both the sun goddess, Amaterasu (the divine ancestor of the imperial house, see p.28), and the harvest goddess, Toyouke, acquire renewed vigor, and this also ensures the continuing vitality of both the imperial line and the rice crop, without either of which it would be impossible for the nation to survive.

At the end of the twenty-year cycle, the new shrine buildings are erected on a site alongside the old ones. For a brief period, the visitor might be forgiven for experiencing a sense of double vision, because the complex and its copy stand side-by-side until the sacred images have been ritually transferred to the new shrine by the distinctively clad Ise priests. Only then are the old structures dismantled and the ground cleared, to be carefully maintained until the rebuilding cycle comes around again.

The dismantled buildings continue to be imbued with the powerful sacred essence of the goddesses and are not destroyed. Instead, pieces are distributed to shrines throughout Japan and incorporated into their walls, thereby spiritually reinvigorating the entire Shinto universe. The new structures are built by carpenters who typically come from families who have participated in this activity for generations. Thus, the Ise shrines are steeped in ancient tradition, but at the same time always appear new and fresh.

Articles VII and XVII from Shotoku's Constitution

" VII. Let every man have his own charge, and let not the spheres of duty be confused. When wise men are entrusted with office, the sound of praise arises. If unprincipled men hold office, disasters and tumults are multiplied. In this world, few are born with knowledge: wisdom is the product of earnest meditation. In all things, whether great or small, find the right man, and they will surely be well managed: on all occasions, be they urgent or the reverse, meet but with a wise man, and they will of themselves be amenable. In this way will the State be lasting and the Temples of the Earth and of Grain will be free from danger. Therefore did the wise sovereigns of antiquity seek the man to fill the office, and not the office for the sake of the man. "

" XVII. Decisions on important matters should not be made by one person alone. They should be discussed with many. But small matters are of less consequence. It is unnecessary to consult a number of people. It is only in the case of the discussion of weighty affairs, when there is a suspicion that they may miscarry, that one should arrange matters in concert with others, so as to arrive at the right conclusion. "

Cited in *Sources of Japanese Tradition*, edited by Tsunoda, Rusaku., et al. Columbia University Press: New York, 1958, p.50–53.

Commentary

Shotoku-Taishi's "Seventeen-Article Constitution" (604CE) is arguably the most important single document in Japanese history, because it established the foundation for all subsequent articulations of Japanese ethical and moral principles. Although it is grounded in the Confucian ideology that the prince had so assiduously studied, the constitution also expresses a uniquely Japanese concern with the establishment and maintenance of *wa* ("benign harmony").

Article VII stresses the importance of seeking wise men to hold office, and of fostering a hierarchical order in which the "spheres of duty" are clearly delimited. Article XVII stresses the necessity of collective decision-making, especially when it comes to "weighty affairs." This is a principle that still guides Japanese decision-making, and was applied in the decision on the part of the *sodaikai* ("shrine elders' association") to allow young women to carry the *mikoshi* in the Tokyo neighborhood of Nishi-Waseda (see p.82 and p.99). Indeed, it has been said that the constitution introduced by Shotoku-Taishi could easily serve as the charter for a modern Japanese corporation.

金星大神
奉
納
昭和三年
奉
加古川市
畑 良明
納
昭和六十一年一月十二日建之
鳴瀬良彦

CHAPTER SIX

SACRED SPACE

Although, according to Shinto, all of Japan may be considered a "sacred space," the focal point of worship is the *jinja*, or shrine, where one or more *kami* are enshrined. Distinguishable from Buddhist temples, or *otera*, by the presence of sacred gateways known as *torii*, these *jinja*s range in size and importance from tiny enclaves on the roofs of modern high-rise buildings in big cities to the Naiku and Geku—the "Inner" and "Outer" shrines at Ise—and the massive Meiji-*jingu* in Tokyo, which is dedicated to the spirit of Emperor Meiji (reigned 1867–1912).

In addition to these hallowed precincts, where worshipers celebrate and practice their faith, the Shinto tradition considers some features of the natural landscape, such as Mount Fuji, or Fuji-*san* (revered as a deity in its own right), to be equally sacred.

LEFT: Fox figures guard the shrine of the rice god, Inari, at Fushimi, near Kyoto—it is the largest of more than 40,000 shrines in Japan dedicated to the god. The fox is both Inari's guardian and messenger.

Shinto has always been a highly personal and local religion, except during the period in which it became established as the state cult (see p.18). Its *jinja*, or shrines, dedicated to countlesss *kami* ("spirits"; see pp.24–5), are scattered throughout Japan, and, because these beings are believed to animate features of the environment, many natural places are also considered sacred in the Shinto faith.

The typical Shinto *jinja* is a complex of several buildings, and, with the exception of the tiny shrines sometimes found on the roofs of domestic structures, they are almost always located in natural settings, even if this is only a few trees shading an urban open space.

Because Shinto is such an ancient tradition, its shrines reflect the evolution of Japanese history and technology. The earliest *jinja* were simple outdoor altars, often carved from local rock, upon which offerings could be laid. As time went on, these sacred open-air precincts—frequently constructed around a revered natural object such as a tree or stone—were enclosed and the new structures came to resemble the ceramic storehouses of the Yayoi culture (see pp.14–15). Many of the enclosed shrines were used for the veneration of rice deities and were modeled on thatched rice storehouses. The two most ancient Shinto shrines are also the most sacred—those of Ise and Izumo. Dedicated to the patron god of the Izumo region, Okuninushi (see pp.29–30), the "Great Lord of the Country," the *jinja* at Izumo is built of wood and thatch and, like Ise, has been rebuilt frequently to an identical design.

The Grand Shrines at Ise (see pp.62–3) stand next to the Isuzu River. The complex is dedicated to two major divinities and has been the destination of Japanese pilgrims for over a millennium. The site's most ancient shrine—and Shinto's holiest place—is the Naiku ("Inner Shrine"), dedicated to the sun goddess Amaterasu. The site also includes the Geku ("Outer Shrine") of the goddess of the harvest, Toyouke. Amaterasu holds the sacred mirror, a prime symbol of the sun goddess and one of three imperial talismans, which were supposedly brought to Earth by Amaterasu's grandson Honinigi (see p.29). The Japanese emperor traditionally makes an annual pilgrimage to the Naiku to report the year's events to his divine ancestor as well as to pray for a good year's rice crop.

Ise is distinguished from all other Shinto shrines by the fact that it is completely torn down and then rebuilt every twenty years (see pp.62–3). This custom, which began in the eighth century CE, serves, by extension, to renew the enshrined divinities.

During the Nara period (710–94CE), many Shinto shrines were transformed due to the influence of Buddhism. Not only did Shinto theology adapt to the alien faith, but also its shrine architecture began to incorporate elements of Chinese design, such as upturned gables, elaborate ornamentation, and bright vermilion paint instead of natural wood—such aspects marked a significant departure from the simplicity of Ise.

An important early example of the new Chinese style is the Kasuga-*jinja* in Nara. From this time on, the Shinto *jinja* and Buddhist *otera* came to look very similar. However, just as the presence of a *pagoda* is a common means of identifying an *otera*, the *jinja* is instantly recognizable by its ceremonial *torii*, or sacred gateway, which is usually festooned with *gohei*—paired strips of paper, each torn in four places to symbolize the presence of *kami*.

In its simplest form, as at Ise, the *torii* consists of a pair of posts topped by two crossbars, one of which extends beyond the uprights. The *torii* serves to mark the boundary between the impure, outer, secular world and the sacred confines of the shrine. In passing through it, a visitor to the shrine symbolically undergoes a ritual purification of the pollution accumulated in the outer world. Japan's most famous *torii* is in the sea off

An 18th-century woodblock print depicting Ise, the most sacred shrine complex in Japan, attended by visitors. The emperor presides over annual rituals at Ise, and only the imperial family and Shinto priests can enter the sacred precincts of the Naiku ("Inner Shrine").

the island of Miyajima and marks the entrance to the shrine of Itsukushima (see illustration, p.2). Visitors must pass through the gateway by boat before entering the shrine.

Beyond the *torii*, the *jinja*—whether it be a vast complex, such as the Meiji-*jingu* in Tokyo and the Heian shrine in Kyoto, or a tiny rooftop shrine—will follow a fundamentally standard layout. Typically it is composed of two principal elements: the *honden* ("sanctuary"), which holds the image of the *kami* to which the shrine is dedicated and is rarely, if ever, visited by laypeople, and the *haiden* ("oratory"). There will also be one or more storehouses, an outer building before which worshipers pray and make offerings, and a stone trough containing pure water for the ritual ablutions required before one ventures near the image of the *kami* (see p.62).

Once purified, the worshiper approaches the *haiden*, makes a small monetary offering, and either rings a bell attached to a long rope or claps twice (or both) to attract the attention of the *kami*. He or she then bows, pressing the hands together in an attitude of prayer, and silently asks a favor of the *kami*. When the request has been made, the worshiper claps to signal the end of the prayer. If the favor is granted, the petitioner is expected to return to thank the *kami*.

Larger shrines typically have a public meeting hall, a stage for ritual performances, one or more storehouses, in which *mikoshi* ("portable shrines") are kept between festivals, and stalls where *miko* ("shrine virgins") sell good-luck charms and personal fortunes. If the buyer approves of the fortune, they will tie it to a tree in the grounds so that the local god may take note of it.

The Shinto shrine serves as the focus of a great many rituals and associated activities (see pp.61–3). Personal requests are the most ubiquitous form of religious observance in Shinto, but the most important time is when the local *kami* is feted by the community.

All Shinto shrines are managed by groups of lay people who pay the *guji* and *kannushi*—the head priest and the other priests—and generally oversee the affairs of the shrine. Some major shrines, such as Tokyo's Meiji-*jingu*, have dozens of priests, whereas smaller neighborhood *jinja* often have no full-time *guji* and the tasks of one are generally performed by a *sodai*, a lay member of the *sodaikai* ("shrine elders' association").

Every traditional Japanese family home has a miniature shrine, or *kamidana* (literally, a "god-shelf"). This contains a small replica of a *honden* with the names of family ancestors who are honored as *kami*. An elderly member of the household, often the grandmother, tends the *kamidana* by placing on it each morning small cups of *saké*, or rice wine, and dishes containing a few grains of rice and vegetables. Priests distribute similar offerings at shrines, because all *kami* must be nourished if they are to perform at peak efficiency.

As far as the natural landscape is concerned, a reverence for mountains and a fascination with their sanctity has long been a marked feature of Shinto. The most famous of all Japanese sacred mountains is Mount Fuji, or Fuji-*san*, which is traditionally considered an important *kami* in its own right. It has long been a place of mass pilgrimage, and each year thousands of devotees climb it to worship at the small shrine at the summit—an act that is, in effect, a performance of worship. In the nineteenth century, when travel was more difficult, a "Fuji cult" developed that involved erecting small replicas of the mountain at local Shinto *jinja* in many parts of Japan. Those unable to climb the real mountain would walk up the replica in a symbolic act of pilgrimage.

It may be no coincidence that as Shinto shrines adopted more Chinese architectural characteristics in the Nara period, and thus came to resemble Buddhist temples in appearance (see p.70), the process of syncretism between the two faiths proceeded accordingly. Indeed, almost every major Buddhist *otera* includes at least one small Shinto *jinja*. A curious result of this process was the movement known as Shugendo ("Way of the Mountain"), which took shape in the Heian period (794–1185CE). Spread by mystics known as *yamabushi* (literally, "mountain warriors"), it involved a fusion of Buddhist *bosatsu* ("enlightened beings") and Shinto *kami* (see p.24), especially the *kami* believed to live on mountains. Shugendo survives to this day in parts of northern Japan and is practiced in sacred buildings that are at once *otera* and *jinja*.

In addition to mountains, countless other natural features are also held to be sacred. Indeed, almost every distinctive rock outcrop, river, hill, and waterfall is likely to have some association with a local temple, shrine, or both. Examples include the magnificent Nachi waterfall in Wakayama prefecture and a spectacular waterfall in Akita, Honshu, both of which, like Fuji-*san*, are widely conceived to be powerful *kami*—deities in their own right—and therefore offer propitious places for worshipers to parade with a *mikoshi* (see illustration, p.26). Whole regions are also considered sacred because of their association with particular Shinto deities. For example, the Yamato region is revered as the homeland of the imperial dynasty which, according to Shinto myth, is of divine descent (see p.38).

The Holy Place of Amaterasu

“3rd month, 10th day. Amaterasu no Oho-kami [Amaterasu] was taken from [the princess] Toyo-suki-iri-hime no Mikoto, and entrusted to [the princess] Yamato-hime no Mikoto. Now Yamato-hime no Mikoto sought for a place where she might enshrine the Great Goddess. So she proceeded to Sasahata in Uda. Then turning back from thence, she entered the land of Ohomi, and went round eastwards to Mino, whence she arrived in the province of Ise.

Now Amaterasu no Oho-kami instructed Yamato-hime no Mikoto, saying: 'The province of Ise, of the divine wind, is the land whither repair the waves from the eternal world, the successive waves. It is a secluded and pleasant land. In this land I wish to dwell.'
In compliance, therefore, with the instruction of the Great Goddess, a shrine was erected to her in the province of Ise. Accordingly an Abstinence Palace was built at Kaha-kami in Isuzu. This was called the palace of Iso. It was there that Amaterasu no Oho-kami first descended from Heaven.”

From *Nihongi, Chronicles of Japan from the Earliest Times to A.D. 697. Vol 1*, translated by W.G. Aston. Kegan Paul, Trench, Trübner & Co. Limited: London, 1896, p.176.

Commentary

Ise, the site of the Grand Shrine of the sun goddess Amaterasu (to give her name in its simplified English form), is the most sacred location in the Shinto religion. As this passage from the *Nihonshoki* indicates, the goddess was originally in the care of a princess named Toyo-suki-iri-hime. But according to the chronicle, around the beginning of the Common Era she was entrusted to a royal princess called Yamato-hime and enshrined in what is now the Naiku ("Inner Shrine") at Ise, near the coast southeast of Nara in Mie prefecture, Honshu. Indeed, the *Nihonshoki* asserts that Amaterasu herself selected the location, because it was where she first descended to Earth.

Yamato-hime became the first High Priestess of Ise, a role that was eventually absorbed by male priests, although early accounts of figures such as Yamato-hime have been drawn upon to justify an expanded role for women in modern Shinto. The High Priestess's residence was called the "Abstinence Palace," because custom dictated that she must remain unmarried while she served Amaterasu. It was not until the eighth century CE that the practice of rebuilding the Ise shrines at twenty-year intervals was established. The next rebuilding will take place in 2013.

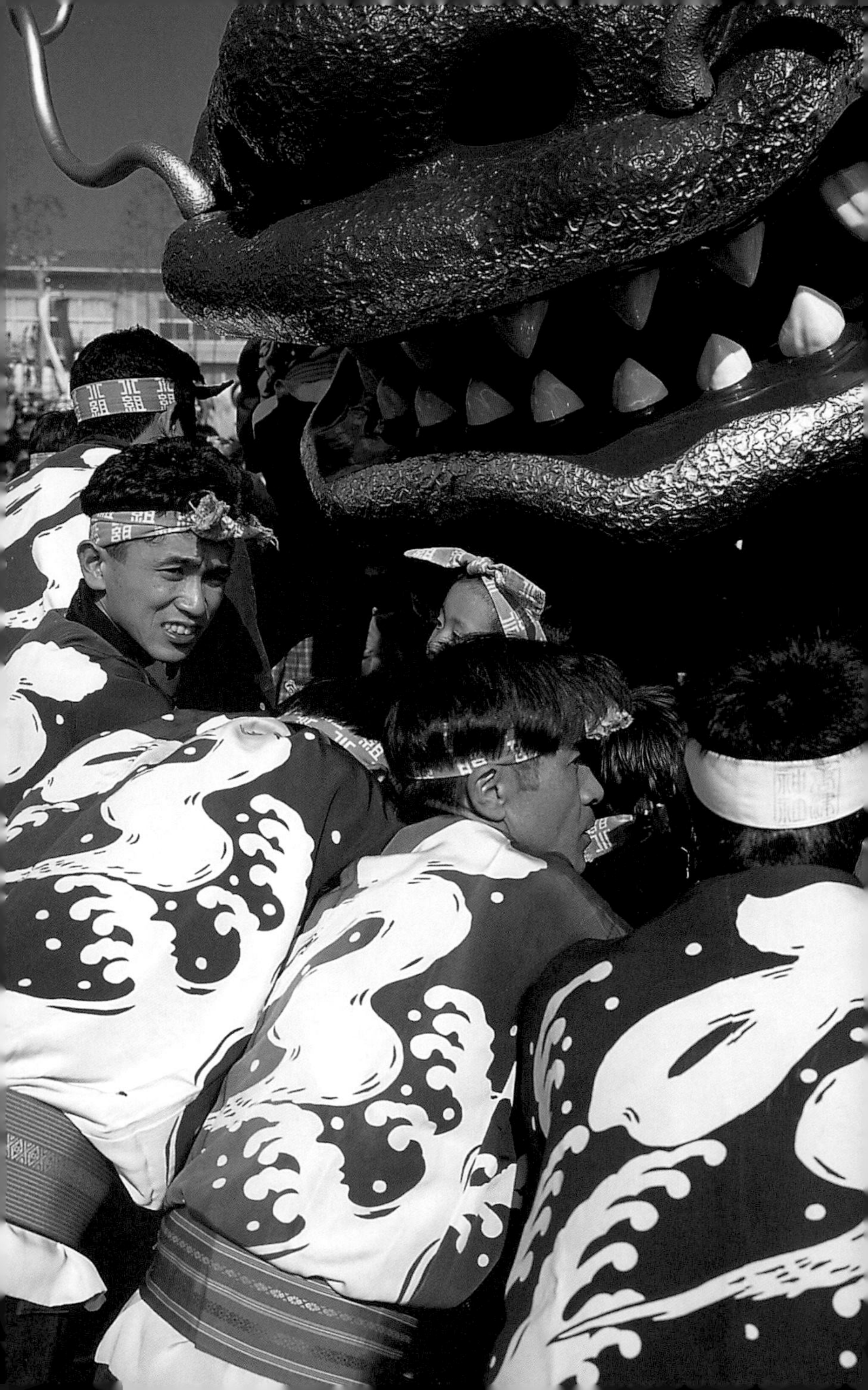

CHAPTER SEVEN

SACRED TIME

The Shinto calendar has a great abundance of local festivals and rituals. Some of these, such as Obon, the annual festival honoring the souls of the dead, and Shogatsu Matsuri, the three-day New Year's festival, overlap with Buddhist rituals, while others are purely Shinto-based.

These practices provide a channel through which human beings are able to communicate with the divine realm and, in the process, maintain both their own and their community's well-being. Examples of local Shinto rituals include petitioning the *kami* to grant good health, prosperity, and success; tending the family *kamidana* ("household shrine"); and participating in a *matsuri* ("festival"), in which a *mikoshi* ("portable shrine") is carried through a village or neighborhood, thereby sanctifying both the carriers and the community as a whole.

LEFT: An enormous lacquered fish is hauled through the streets of Karatsu on Kyushu island during the city's annual Kunchi matsuri. *Giant colorful floats of various creatures are a feature of this 300-year-old festival.*

The three-day Japanese New Year festival, Shogatsu Matsuri, has been celebrated from January 1 to January 3 since Japan abandoned the Chinese lunar calendar in favor of the Gregorian on January 1, 1873. In the days immediately preceding the New Year, houses are cleaned thoroughly in order to begin the year unpolluted. During the festival, family meals include a special soup (*ozoni*) and pounded rice cakes (*mochi*); and gifts are given to superiors as tokens of appreciation.

But the most important activity of Shogatsu Matsuri is a visit to a shrine or temple to make an offering and pray for prosperity and good health in the coming months. In some sects, miniature household shrines and the tablets bearing the names of family ancestors are ritually burned and replaced with new ones.

One of the most widely conducted of all Japanese festivals is Obon, the Buddhist celebration of the annual return of the dead to their ancestral homes in mid-August (the date is still determined by the lunar calendar). Many people visit their hometowns at this time to clean family gravestones. They also say prayers for the dead, especially the newly departed, and join in *bon-odori*, a traditional Shinto dance to honor the deceased.

At other times of the year, regular ancestor rites take place in the home. From the Shinto standpoint, the souls of the dead take on the status of a low level of deity; from the Buddhist perspective, they are seen as souls seeking salvation. But both concepts are accepted, reflecting Japanese "ambiguity tolerance" in spiritual matters.

Some domestic ancestor rituals, especially during Obon, involve burning incense on the *butsudan*, or domestic Buddhist altar, and offering small dishes of rice to the souls of the family's ancestors. Seven days after death, the soul is given a *kaimyo* ("death-name") that is inscribed on one of the *ihai*, or ancestral tablets, kept in the *butsudan*. The same ancestral souls are also revered as Shinto *tama* (see p.90) or *kami*, represented by tablets on the *kamidana* ("household shrine" or domestic "god-shelf"), often directly above the *butsudan*. Offerings are also made to these family *kami*. Most domestic rites are performed in the early morning, a time considered sacred in both Buddhism and Shinto.

As far as most communities are concerned, by far the most important Shinto ritual is the annual (or, in some cases, biennial) local *matsuri* ("festival"). Virtually every Japanese town, neighborhood, village, or *buraku* ("village quarter") has such a festival, which centers on the shrine to the local Shinto *kami*. There are two basic types of *matsuri*. The first, an "ordinary festival," or "shadow *matsuri*," does not directly involve the local *kami*, but is still centered on the shrine, and culminates in the festive procession of a *mikoshi* ("portable shrine"), around the neighborhood. The second type of *matsuri* is a *taisai* ("big festival"), during which the *mikoshi* contains the sacred image of the local *kami*. In both types of *matsuri*, the three groupings that represent the local community—the *shotenkai* ("merchants' association"), the *chokai* ("neighborhood residents' association"), and the *sodaikai* ("shrine elders' association")—present a positive image of the locality, and at the same time reinforce their own sense of social solidarity and local pride.

The *matsuri* celebrated in the 3rd *chome* ("district") of Nishi-Waseda, a northwest Tokyo neighborhood, is a triennial *taisai* in honor of the sun goddess Amaterasu, who is the *kami* of the local shrine, the Tenso-*jinja*. It is one of thousands of smaller shrines to the goddess found throughout Japan, the most important being at Ise (see p.62, p.69 and pp.76–7).

The *matsuri* traditionally takes place over a two-day period in early September. On the morning of the first day, children carry a small *mikoshi* around the neighborhood. In the afternoon, assisted by the local *sodai* ("shrine elders"), the acting *guji* (the senior Shinto priest, as opposed to a *kannushi* or ordinary priest) chants Shinto prayers and purifies the shrine and its contents by

A miko *("shrine virgin"; see p.62) performs a* kagura *dance—one that celebrates the renewal of life.*

waving a *sakaki*, or branch of sacred pine tree. In the evening, there is public entertainment in the grounds of the shrine.

Early the next morning the *guji* removes the sacred (and rarely seen) image of Amaterasu from the inner precincts of the shrine and places it in the waiting *mikoshi*. In rotation, teams of young men and women then carry it along the narrow street, chanting "*Wa shoi! Wa shoi!*" (a cry similar to "Hurrah!"). The procession is led by the *guji* and includes singers, a drummer, a young man impersonating a *tengu*—the guardian of the shrine—and the *sodai*. Once the procession has returned to the grounds of the shrine, the priest removes the image from the *mikoshi* and returns it to its place in the inner shrine, where it will remain until the next *taisai*.

The fundamental purpose of this ritual is to sanctify the neighborhood served by the *jinja* by periodically exposing it to the sacred aura emitted by the divine image paraded in the *mikoshi*, which also, of course, sanctifies the *mikoshi*-bearers. A *matsuri* is therefore a joyous occasion, one in which the participants feel that they partake of the divine essence of the local *kami*. In the process, they may experience feelings close to ecstasy.

In addition to participating in communal household rites and local festivals, a great many Japanese go to temples and shrines individually to seek the blessings of the local *bosatsu* ("enlightened being") or *kami* (see p.31), especially when faced with some personal crisis. Requests might include asking the *kami* to heal a sick infant or ensure the fertility of a marriage.

One of the most common Shinto rites of passage is the birth ritual known as *omiyamairi* (literally "honorable shrine visit"—*omiya* being a synonym for *jinja*), when the infant is welcomed into the community of its family. Some months after the birth, the parents take the child to a shrine to be purified by the *kannushi*. Typically, the child's extended family are also present, and afterward there is a festive meal.

Ritual purification is a highly significant aspect of most Shinto ceremonies (see also pp.61–3). Brandishing the *sakaki* (see p.84) and chanting appropriate *norito*, or prayers, the *guji* or *kannushi* seeks to remove any spiritual pollution contaminating the person, place, or thing. Such pollution can include possession by *oni* ("demons"; see p.25).

Purification of the bride and groom is central to traditional Japanese wedding ceremonies, which are typically performed by Shinto priests. However, for the most part these take place not at shrines but in hotels and purpose-built "wedding palaces."

The Silent *Matsuri* in Yuzawa

“The *mikoshi* part of the parade, the *shinko shiki*, consists of the *kami*'s badges of rank, attendants, paraphernalia, priests, escort, shrine maidens, and the *mikoshi* itself, which carries the *kami*'s *shintai* [the sacred image that is placed in the *mikoshi* before the parade commences]. The *mikoshi* of the Atago-*jinja* is a massive structure carried silently through the streets, in contrast to rowdy Kanto practice. It is preceded by boys carrying baskets into which spectators put offerings of bags of rice and coins. The *mikoshi* is followed by the *mikoshi* guardians, two representatives from each of the Go Cho, dressed in *montsuki* (formal traditional dress), and the representatives of the first families who worshiped the *shintai*. The *guji* (chief priest) of Atago-*jinja* and his assistant, a *guji* in his own right of a neighboring village shrine, ride in *jinriksha*, and the other officiant *kannushi* for the ritual follow on foot. The shrine maidens ride flower-bedecked carts, and *sakaki* carriers, *sambo* (footed trays for offerings) carriers, and porters march on foot.”

From *Matsuri: Festivals of a Japanese Town* by Michael Ashkenazi. University of Hawaii Press: Honolulu, 1993, p.57.

Commentary

This account of a modern *matsuri* procession comes from Michael Ashkenazi, a well-known contemporary anthropologist who has studied the festivals in Yuzawa, a small town in northern Japan. He is describing the *gyoretsu* ("parade"), in which the Atago-*jinja*'s *mikoshi* is carried through the streets of the town every year. The order of marching is important, because it reflects the local Shinto hierarchy. Thus, the *mikoshi* is closely followed by senior representatives of the Go Cho, the five neighborhoods that constitute what would in the West be called the Atago-*jinja*'s "parish," while the *guji* (the senior priest) and his assistant come next, riding in rickshaws. Other priests follow on foot. The *miko* ("shrine virgins") ride in carts, a feature that is unique to this *matsuri*. A big difference between the parade in Yuzawa and those witnessed by the author of this book is the silence—quite a shock compared to the loud and rhythmic shouts of "*Wa shoi!*" that characterize *gyoretsu* in the Tokyo area (see pp.82–4). Although the processions held throughout Japan all contain familiar aspects, each *matsuri* also has elements that are unique to its particular location.

CHAPTER EIGHT

DEATH AND THE AFTERLIFE

Unlike most world religions, Shinto—an essentially life-affirming creed—places little emphasis on death and the afterlife. Its followers tend to look elsewhere, primarily to Buddhist conceptions of the afterworld, for comfort when faced with the prospect of death or the passing of a loved one. Indeed, although most Japanese are married according to Shinto rites (see p.85), only a tiny minority, which includes the imperial family, are buried in Shinto cemeteries.

However, according to Shinto belief, the *tama* ("soul") of the deceased continues to exert an influence on the living before it finally merges with the *kami* ancestors from the family of which it was a part. The Shinto conception of the afterlife thus reflects the Japanese emphasis on continuity over the generations and the collective identity of family and clan.

LEFT: Sacred straw ropes and paper cuttings known as gohei, *which indicate that these gravestone markers in woodland are to be treated with reverence.*

Shinto is essentially a "life religion" and is primarily concerned with the here and now, the abundance of nature, and human and animal fertility. Since the advent of Buddhism, specifically Shinto ideas of life after death and the salvation of the soul have become confined to the belief that a person's spirit persists after death and remains effective for the benefit of the living. The *tama* ("ancestral souls") are considered part of the social group to whom one is duty-bound not to fall into a state of shame (see pp.58–9). The *tama* of the newly deceased are therefore nourished with offerings at the *kamidana* ("family shrine"; see p.81); in return, they are expected to bless and protect the living.

Japan's prehistoric religion appears to have had a well-developed concept of an afterlife. A great deal of attention was paid to the disposition of the body, and during the Kofun period (ca. 300–552CE), elaborate tumuli were constructed to house the spirits of dead emperors. Ancient Shinto does seem to have possessed the concept of a Hades-like infernal region, as seen in the image of Yomi in the *Kojiki* (see p.94), but save for the celebrated episode in which Izanagi visits this subterranean realm in a vain attempt to retrieve his dead spouse (see p.41), there is no further mention of the place and it plays no role in modern Shinto theology.

Buddhist ideas have for the most part superseded Shinto concepts of regions of the dead—but not entirely. After thirty-three years, the *tama* is believed to lose its individual nature and to merge with the collective body of family *kami*. These ancestral spirits are said to dwell on a sacred mountain, often situated in the Kumano, Yoshino, or another mountainous region of the heartland of ancient Japan. The amorphous family *kami* are also invoked in ritual, but at a more abstract level than the *tama* of a family member who has recently passed away.

The Buddhist sects introduced a number of afterworld concepts, including paradisial regions presided over by the Buddha himself (the "Pure Land" and Nichiren sects), the Vairocana Buddha (the Shingon sect), the Maitreya, and Kannon. They also introduced the concept of divine judgment, in which, forty-nine days after death, the soul is assessed by a being called Emma (Sanskrit Yama). Depending on his judgment, the soul is assigned either to a paradise, or to one of the demonic regions of Jigoku (hell), or to rebirth as a beast, a deity, or a new human being. However, the most pervasive Buddhist afterworld concept was that of the "Pure Land," a paradise where souls could escape the torments of Jigoku and achieve *nirvana* (see p.60).

Most Japanese see no conflict in embracing both the Shintoist belief in the soul as both *tama* and *kami* and the Buddhist belief that the soul is assigned to hell or paradise and reincarnation, however contradictory the notions may at first appear.

Today the great majority of Japanese choose to be cremated with Buddhist rites and to have their ashes interred in a Buddhist cemetery. Almost all Japanese cemeteries are attached to temples, especially those of the "Pure Land" sects (Jodo-shu and Jodo-shinshu). However, it is possible to be buried according to Shinto rites, and there are at least two Shinto cemeteries in Tokyo. One of them is reserved for the imperial family, whose funerals are traditionally Shinto in form. The most recent was that of the late Showa emperor (Hirohito) in 1989, which was presided over by Shinto priests from Ise (see p.69) and other important shrines.

Shinto also encompasses a widespread folk belief in *obake* (ghosts)—restless spirits who, in life, suffered at the hands of others and thirst for revenge, or who died under less than honorable circumstances. A good example of this phenomenon can be seen in the post-mortem career of Sugawara no Michizane (see pp.32–3), a ninth-century Heian (Kyoto) courtier who was unjustly accused of misconduct in office and who later died in

Mount Fuji is the pre-eminent sacred mountain in Japan and is one of the places where family spirits are said to gather.

exile from his beloved city. His vengeful *obake* caused numerous plagues and other catastrophes until he was enshrined as the *kami* Tenjin.

Of course, not every restless *obake* is enshrined, and most continue to haunt the living as they act out their anger and frustration. Indeed, most contemporary Japanese amusement parks include an "*obake* house," in which ghostly images provide the same kind of delicious thrills one experiences in a Western "haunted house" at Halloween.

The Japanese Realm of the Dead

“The old legends that dead souls go to Yomi cannot be proven. Then it may be asked, where do the souls of the Japanese go when they die? It may be clearly seen from the purport of ancient legends and from modern examples that they remain eternally in Japan and serve in the realm of the dead governed by Okuninushi-no-kami. This realm of the dead is not in any one particular place in the visible world, but being a realm of the darkness and separated from the present world, it cannot be seen....

The darkness, however, is only comparative. It should not mistakenly be imagined that this realm is devoid of light. It has food, clothing, and houses of various kinds, similar to those of the visible world. Proof of this may be found in accounts ... in which a person has occasionally returned to tell of the realm of the dead.

After death the soul leaves the body and resides in the area of the grave, a fact attested by countless accounts ... of both ancient and modern times of miraculous occurrences by spirits in the vicinity of graves.... Some say that the soul goes to the filthy realm of Yomi, but there is not a shred of evidence that this is the case.”

Cited in *Sources of Japanese Tradition*, edited by Tsunoda, Rusaku., et al. Columbia University Press: New York, 1958,.p.550.

Commentary

Hirata Atsutane (see p.35) here disputes the belief that the souls of the dead go to Yomi, the primordial land of the dead, from which Izanagi vainly attempted to extract his dead wife Izanami (see p.41). Rather, Hirata suggests that the dead remain in an invisible (and non-localized) realm, one that is governed by Okuninushi, the "Great Lord of the Country" (see pp.28–9), but is nevertheless firmly connected to the Japanese mortal realm.

The Shinto scholar goes on to assert that the afterworld is similar to the mortal realm and that because it cannot be seen from the mortal world, it is often erroneously thought to be a dark place. Despite Hirata's attempt to describe a Shinto afterworld, few modern Japanese put much stock in the presence of such a realm. Indeed, the overwhelming majority are buried according to Buddhist rites. Shinto, with its emphasis on this world, has never made much of the nature of "life" after an earthly existence. In the *Kojiki* and *Nihonshoki*, the dark and filthy realm of Yomi is associated with the uncleanliness of death—the decomposition and putrefaction that ceasing to exist in bodily form entails. In Shinto, the practical importance of ritual ablutions to restore purity seems to affirm its remoteness from death.

CHAPTER NINE

SOCIETY AND RELIGION

The Shinto faith has undergone some major changes in the modern period: from its status as a state-sponsored cult between 1871 and 1945, it has, since the end of the Second World War, been transformed into what amounts to a congregational religion. In the course of the last two hundred years, it has also given rise to a large number of sects. Some of these, such as Tenrikyo, command the devotion of millions of Japanese worshipers; while others—for example, Shukyo Mahikari—have a mere handful of followers.

Shinto's movement into the modern age is perhaps most clearly witnessed by the increasing number of women being permitted entry into the priesthood, and by the agreement to allow young women to carry *mikoshi* ("portable shrines") during festivals.

LEFT: A bride poses for her Shinto wedding portrait. The dress is traditional and includes the elaborate hairstyle and the women's overcoat or uchikake.

For centuries, women have played a relatively minor role in Japan's religious life, despite the existence of high priestesses of Ise (see p.77) and the fact that there were reigning empresses until well into the early historic period. But around 800CE the impact of Chinese Confucianism and its heavily patriarchal ideology effectively put an end to this early equality. Since that time, all emperors and most priests have been male, even though Amaterasu remains Shinto's most revered deity.

In recent years, the women's movement has begun to exert an influence on traditional Japanese beliefs and practices. There has also been an increase in the number of women Shinto priests, in spite of opposition from the more conservative shrines—in the late 1990s, out of 21,091 priests, ten percent were women, compared with nine percent in 1993—and an increasing number of Shinto shrines now permit young women to carry *mikoshi* ("portable shrines") during festivals.

The act of carrying the *mikoshi* during a *matsuri* ("festival"; see pp.82–4) is regarded as a considerable privilege, especially on those occasions when the *mikoshi* contains the image of the deity from the local Shinto shrine. Traditionally, the task of *mikoshi*-bearing was reserved for young men—women were expected to play a supportive role in *matsuri* processions, providing refreshments for *mikoshi*-bearers and cooking dinner after the *mikoshi* had been returned to the main shrine.

However, this situation began to change in the late 1970s, with women gradually gaining the right to join their menfolk in carrying the *kami* through the streets. In the Tokyo neighborhood of Nishi-Waseda (see p.82), this change occurred in 1978. The *guji* ("chief priest") who approved the change, cited as a precedent the fact that there were once high priestesses of Amaterasu at Ise—Amaterasu is also the local deity of Nishi-Waseda.

However, in other areas it has proved more difficult to break from the past: Shinto's former association with the state militarism that existed until 1945 still causes controversy in the context of the Yasukuni shrine in Tokyo. The *kami* enshrined in this *jinja* are the souls of Japan's war dead from the creation of the Japanese Imperial Army in 1871 to the end of the Second World War. The shrine thus continues to be the topic of considerable debate, particularly when prominent members of the government—sometimes even the prime minister—call to pay their respects. (While the Buddhist sects have generally steered clear of politics, they have also been less responsive to the kind of pressure for change that has led to women entering the Shinto priesthood. Japanese Buddhism has few, if any, women priests.)

Although such occurrences at Yasukuni may not be frequent, they always receive significant coverage in the Japanese media. The Left, evoking prewar "State Shinto" and its intensely nationalist ideology, accuses the politicians involved of violating Japan's 1947 constitution, which clearly prohibits the state from involvement in any religion. The Right counters with the claim that the Yasukuni shrine is a private religious institution and that those who pray there do so as private individuals. Complicating matters is the fact that in recent years there have been repeated attempts to turn the Yasukuni-*jinja* into Japan's equivalent of a "tomb of the unknown soldier," a place where visiting foreign dignitaries may lay wreaths. But the sensitivities of the Left on this issue resonate across much of the Japanese political spectrum and, so far, the measure has failed to receive sufficient backing in the Japanese Diet (parliament).

Since the early nineteenth century, Japan has spawned a host of spiritual movements that have collectively come to be referred to as the Shinko Shukyo ("New Religions"). The great majority of these are derivatives of Shinto, although most are heavily infused with ideas drawn from a variety of sources, including Buddhism, Chinese traditions such as Confucianism and Daoism, Christianity, and, in modern times, even Western occultism. Despite occasional excesses and sometimes garbled theological underpinnings, the Shinko Shukyo provide evidence that the ancient impetus to religious innovation is very much alive in modern Japan.

The first Shinko Shukyo arose against the background of growing social chaos that accompanied the breakdown of the Tokugawa shogunate (1603–1867). At this time, a number of successful new sects sprang up,

A procession of formally attired Shinto priests with their distinctive kanmuri *headgear at the Meiji shrine in Tokyo.*

usually led by charismatic individuals. Their success continued in the Meiji period (1868–1912), by the end of which thirteen Shinto-based sects had been recognized by the Japanese government. One of these was the Tenrikyo ("Heavenly Truth") sect founded in 1838 by a farmer's wife named Miki Nakayama (see pp.50–51). Today, from its headquarters in Tenri City, just south of Nara, it claims a membership of almost two million people. Although it is primarily rooted in the Shinto concept of a hierarchy of *kami*, the religion incorporates concepts borrowed from "Pure Land" Buddhism, including the concept of "salvation" and a well-defined afterworld. The Tenrikyo faith has been carried to Hawaii, North America, Brazil, and other countries with sizeable Japanese immigrant populations.

Several movements have also arisen directly from Buddhist traditions, the most influential being Soka Gakkai ("Value Creating Society"), founded in the 1920s by Makiguchi Tsuesaburo (1871–1944) and closely linked to the Nichiren-shoshu sect. By the Second World War, Tsuesaburo and his disciple Toda Josei (1900–58) had only a few thousand disciples before their devotion to Nichiren's teachings led to their suppression. But after 1945 the movement grew rapidly, spurred by the social upheaval of post-war economic growth.

Soka Gakkai's appeal was primarily to those from rural areas who had migrated to the cities and had lost touch with the social networks that are so important to Japanese life. Attendance at a temple or shrine was based on one's *ie* ("extended family"), so newcomers to an area often found it difficult to join a place of worship. Many Shinko Shukyo arose to meet the spiritual needs of such people, and the more "mainstream" ones, such as Tenrikyo, have come to resemble the older Japanese sects in their promotion of "family values." However, a small minority has been accused of imitating the more notorious cults in the West—for example, through targeting susceptible young people. One such was Aum Shinrikyo, an apocalyptic Buddhist-based sect responsible for a deadly gas attack on the Tokyo metro in 1995.

There are thousands of Shinko Shukyo in Japan today, although many have tiny followings. A good example of a smaller movement is Shukyo Mahikari ("Divine Light"), founded in the early 1960s. It emphasizes the power of healing and has an extraordinarily broad-based theology that draws on Shinto, Buddhism, and a host of other sources. Like other Shinko Shukyo, Shukyo Mahikari demonstrates the continuing vitality of the Japanese genius for blending elements of many different spiritual and cultural traditions.

The Education of Women

“The outward manner and temper of women is rooted in the negative (*yin*) power, and so temperamentally women are apt to be sensitive, petty, narrow, and jaundiced. As they live confined to their homes day in and day out, theirs is a very private life and their vision is quite limited. Consequently, among women compassion and honesty are rare indeed.... It may be added that in ancient times when a girl reached ten years of age, she was turned to a woman-teacher in order to learn the virtues and duties of womanhood. Now that practice has been discontinued, and ‘study’ for women means only a little reading. Completely forgotten is the fact that cultivation of the mind is the essence of all learning. It is because of this that the question now has arisen as to whether or not learning is the business of women. It is imperative that this truth be fully understood, and that great care be given to the proper education of women, lest they should turn out to be the cause of domestic discord and family disaster.”

From *Toju sensei zenshu II* by Toju Nakae cited in *Sources of Japanese Tradition* by Tsunoda, Rusaku., et al. Columbia University Press: New York, 1958, pp.380–81.

Commentary

In this passage from the work of Toju Nakae (1608–48), the author makes a plea for the education of women even though he still accepts the Confucian notion that the "temper of women" is governed by *yin*, perceived as a dark and negative principle, and that "compassion and honesty" are rare among the feminine gender. Nevertheless, Toju urges that women's minds should be cultivated in order to overcome these assumed handicaps, with the ultimate goal being to foster an increase in family *wa* ("benign harmony"; see p.58) by creating ordered and peaceful households.

Despite Toju's seventeenth-century male chauvinism—indeed, his plea is easily perceived as an expression of male self-interest—his request for more education to be provided for women might be considered to represent a small step in the direction of gender equality—though it would be more than three centuries before Japanese women would finally achieve legal parity with men, and full social parity is still an illusive goal.

GLOSSARY

gohei paired strips of paper, each torn into four parts, that symbolize the presence of divinity; can also be made of metal.

guji the chief priest of a shrine.

hokora small sanctuary in the landscape created to honor *kami.*

jinja Shinto shrine.

kami "beings of a higher place," a life-energy recognized by Shinto as existing in all things, both animate and inanimate; the name given to a Shinto deity, god, or spirit. Belief in their existence and according them respect is central to Shinto.

magatama a wondrous jewelled fertility necklace worn by Amaterasu; it is one of three talismans of imperial sovereignty with a sacred mirror and a sword discovered by Susano.

matsuri annual or biennial shrine festival.

miko "shrine virgin," or "altar girl"; in ancient times *miko* were shamans.

mikoshi portable shrine carried around a neighborhood on the shoulders of young people in a *gyoretsu*, or procession.

norito ritual prayers; liturgies.

obake ghosts; restless spirits.

oharai ritual purification prior to worshiping the *kami.*

sakaki sacred pine branch with which purification rites are performed by a *kannushi.*

shirukume a rope made from rice straw which is used as a marker of the presence of *kami*, also called a *shimenawa.*

sodai lay member of a committee that oversees a neighborhood Shinto shrine.

taisai major Shinto shrine festival, in which an image of the *kami* is placed in the *mikoshi*; held every second or third year in most neighborhoods.

tengu benevolent bird-man trickster and guardian; often impersonated to offer protection to the *mikoshi* during a *matsuri.*

Tenno title given to the reigning member of the imperial family during the seventh century, meaning "Heavenly Sovereign."

torii the sacred ceremonial gateway marking the entrance to a Shinto shrine, comprising two slanting upright supports and two cross-pieces, often made of wood and painted vermilion.

wa the concept of "benign harmony," in opposition to chaos.

GENERAL BIBLIOGRAPHY

Ashkenazi, Michael. *Matsuri: Festivals of a Japanese Town*. Honolulu: University of Hawaii Press, 1993.

Aston, W.G. (trans.) *Nihongi, Chronicles of Japan from the Earliest Times to to A.D. 697. Vol 1 and II*. London: Kegan Paul, Trench, Trübner & Co. Limited, 1896.

Blacker, Carmen. *The Catalpa Bow: A Study of Shamanistic Practice in Japan*. London: Allen and Unwin, 1975.

Earhart, H. Byron. *Japanese Religion: Unity and Diversity*. 3rd ed. Belmont, California: Wadsworth, 1983.

Hardacre, Helen. *Shinto and the State, 1868–1988*. Princeton, New Jersey: Princeton University Press, 1989.

Hori, Ichiro. *Folk Religion in Japan: Continuity and Change*. Chicago: University of Chicago Press, 1968.

Kageyama, Haruki. (Christine Guth, trans.) *The Arts of Shinto*. New York and Tokyo: Wheatherill, 1973.

Kato, Genichi. (Christine Guth, trans.) *A Historical Study of the Religious Development of Shinto*. New York: Greenwood Press, 1973.

Littleton, C. Scott. "The Organization and Management of a Shinto Shrine Festival" in *Ethnology 25* (1986): pp.195–202.

Littleton, C. Scott. (ed.) "Shinto" in *Eastern Wisdom: An Illustrated Guide to the Religions and Philosophies of the East*. New York: Henry Holt, 1996.

Mason, J.W.T. *The Meaning of Shinto: The Primaeval Foundation of Creative Spirit in Modern Japan*. New York: Port Kennikat Press, 1965.

McFarland, H. Neil. *The Rush Hour of the Gods: A Study of New Religious Movements of Japan*. New York: Macmillan, 1974.

Nelson, John K. *A Year in the Life of a Shinto Shrine*. Seattle: University of Washington Press, 1996.

Ono, Sokyo. *Shinto: The Kami Way*. Rutland, Vermont: Charles E. Tuttle, 1962.

Philippi, Donald L. (trans.) *Kojiki*. Princeton, New Jersey: Princeton University Press, 1969.

Reader, Ian. *Religion in Contemporary Japan*. Honolulu: University of Hawaii Press, 1991.

Tsunoda, Rusaku, Wm. Theodore de Bary, and Donald Keene. (eds.) *Sources of Japanese Tradition*. New York: Columbia University Press, 1958.

INDEX

Page numbers in **bold** refer to major references; page numbers in *italics* refer to captions

ACKNOWLEDGMENTS AND PICTURE CREDITS

Unless cited otherwise here, text extracts are out of copyright or the product of the author's own translation. The following sources have kindly given their permission.

Origins and Historical Development, p.20: adapted from Tsunoda, R. and Goodrich, L.C. *Japan in the Chinese Dynastic Histories* (1951), pp. 8–16, cited in *Sources of Japanese Tradition*, edited by Tsunoda, Rusaku., et al. Columbia University Press: New York, 1958, pp.6–7.

Aspects of the Divine, p.34: from *Kodo Taii* in *Hirata Atsutane Zenshu I*, pp.22–3, cited in *Sources of Japanese Tradition*, edited by Tsunoda, Rusaku., et al. Columbia University Press: New York, 1958, p.544.

Sacred Texts, p.44:
From *Kojiki*, translated by Donald L. Philippi. Princeton University Press: Princeton, 1969, p.49 and *Nihongi, Chronicles of Japan from the Earliest Times to A.D. 697. Vol 1*, translated by W.G. Aston. Kegan Paul, Trench, Trübner & Co. Limited: London, 1896, pp.10–12.

Sacred Persons, p.54;
Cited in *Sources of Japanese Tradition*, edited by Tsunoda, Rusaku., et al., 1958, p.524.

Ethical Principles, p.64;
Cited in *Sources of Japanese Tradition*, edited by Tsunoda, Rusaku., et al., 1958, p.50–53.

Sacred Space, p.76:
From *Nihongi, Chronicles of Japan from the Earliest Times to A.D. 697. Vol 1*, translated by W.G. Aston. Kegan Paul, Trench, Trübner & Co. Limited: London, 1896, p.176.

Sacred Time, p.86:
From *Matsuri: Festivals of a Japanese Town* by Michael Ashkenazi. University of Hawaii Press: Honolulu, 1993, p.57.

Death and the Afterlife, p.94;
Cited in *Sources of Japanese Tradition*, edited by Tsunoda, Rusaku., et al., 1958, p.550.

Society and Religion, p.104:
From *Toju sensei zenshu II* by Toju Nakae cited in *Sources of Japanese Tradition* by Tsunoda, Rusaku., et al., 1958, pp.380–81.

The publisher would like to thank the following people, museums, and photographic libraries for permission to reproduce their material. Every care has been taken to trace copyright holders. However, if we have omitted anyone we apologize, and will, if informed, make corrections in any future edition.

Page 2 Adina Tovy/Robert Harding, London; **8** C. Rennie/TRIP, Cheam, Surrey; **12** Nigel Blythe/ Robert Harding; **16** Ono Collection, Osaka/ Werner Forman Archive, London; **22** British Museum, London; **26** Ernst Haas/Hulton Archive, London; **36** B.A. Krohn Johansen/ TRIP, Cheam, Surrey; **40–41** Sian Irvine/ DBP; **46** Japan Gallery, London/DBP; **52** Japan Gallery, London/DBP; **58** Abbas/ Magnum Photos, London; **62** Jim Holmes/ Panos Pictures, London; **68** Rainbird/Robert Harding, London; **73** Royal Asiatic Society, London/ DBP; **78** C. Rennie/TRIP, Cheam, Surrey; **83** Michael Macintyre/ Hutchison Library, London; **88** Chris Steele-Perkins/ Magnum Photos, London; **93** Chris Steele-Perkins/ Magnum Photos, London; **96** Michael Macintyre/ Hutchison Library, London; **101** Stock Market/Corbis Images